Happiness, fulfilment, and peacefulness .. .. - -- -----,
one does not look primarily outwards; rather, one looks primarily
inwards. We look inwards to discover our own self; to find the meanings
of our own happiness, to discover what we find fulfilling, and to know
when we are at peace. This journey of "self-discovery" is a life-long
journey that never disappoints; rather, it pleasantly surprises the traveler
with ever new eurekas. It also passes through trials, challenges, and
disappointments, but always concludes in happy and fulfilling
peacefulness.

The spiritual way is so simple and straightforward that I now wonder
why it took me so long and so much effort to find it. One reason is that
one overlooks it, almost dismisses it, because it is so obvious. This
tendency is rather firmly based on experience. All the intricacies of the
religion, all the complexities of the science, all the winding paths of
being street smart, and all the impossible trials of ascetism - these teach
us that the spiritual "way" cannot be so obvious, so simple, and so
happily pleasant. The truth that this traveler discovered is that the
spiritual "way" is indeed obvious, simple, and happily pleasant.

Inner Experiences on the Spiritual Way

Inner Experiences
on the
Spiritual Way

Abdur Rahim Choudhary, Ph.D.

MV Publishers

Published by MV Publishers, a subsidiary of Muslim Voice,
12719 Hillmeade Station Dr, Bowie, MD 20720, USA.
MVPublishers@muslimvoice.org

ISBN 978 1 956601 12 1

First edition 2023
United States of America

Choudhary, Abdur Rahim, 1944–
Inner Experiences on the Spiritual Way

ISBN 978-1-956601-12-1

To the seekers of the Spiritual Way

Content

Preface

I have tried all methods available to me to find the way for a happy, fulfilled and peaceful life. I started with a religious way; then I tried the way of the sciences; then I practiced the ways of the world; and I looked into the ways of the Sufis and the saints, as well as of the bhagats and yogis. None worked for me.

Disappointment that built up gradually prepared the way for the path that actually worked: that is one's personal way. The earlier attempts had not worked, not necessarily because they were false, but because they were external. Happiness, fulfilment, and peacefulness is an internal matter. For that one does not look primarily outwards; rather, one looks primarily inwards. We look inwards to discover our own self; to find the meanings of our own happiness, to discover what we find fulfilling, and to know when we are at peace. This journey of "self-discovery" is a life-long journey that never disappoints; rather, it pleasantly surprises the traveler with ever new eurekas. It also passes through trials, challenges, and disappointments, but always concludes in happy and fulfilling peacefulness.

My personal journey is a long and winding travel. However, it began to take a definitively recognizable shape since 2011. It is now a pleasingly mature theory for the spiritual "way". It is so simple and straightforward that I now wonder why it took me so long and so much effort to find it. One reason is that one overlooks it, almost dismisses it, because it is so obvious. This tendency is rather firmly based on experience. All the intricacies of the religion, all the complexities of the science, all the winding paths of being street smart, and all the impossible trials of ascetism – these teach us that the spiritual "way" cannot be so obvious, so simple, and so happily pleasant. The truth that this traveler discovered is that the spiritual "way" is indeed obvious, simple, and happily pleasant.

I will publish the formulation of the actual theory when it is done. However, I will share almost all the founding elements of the theory in this book.

These elements came to me slowly, gradually, and sometimes after painfully long seeking. As each element came to me, I took personal notes to describe the incidence. The notes were intended for my own consumption as a personal diary. I have collected many such notes and presented them in this book. It includes all the foundational ingredients of the theory for the spiritual "way", such that someone could patiently put these ingredients together, like the pieces in a large Lego construction, and formulate a theory of the spiritual "way".

When these notes were written, being for personal use, they were neither detailed nor self-explanatory. I have included those from among the notes that were relatively easier for general contemplation. I say relatively easier but not necessarily easy. They might need a second reading.

I have refrained from rewriting the material because I wanted to retain the flavor of the content the way it was first written down when the experience was fresh in my mind.

This book is not just the result of research work; it is also the outcome of years of seeking, sessions of meditative contemplation, early morning observations, and thoughts during nature walks. They represent actual happenings and witnessing.

Please feel most welcome to these personal offerings from me.

Abdur Rahim Choudhary
12719 Hillmeade Station Dr, Bowie, MD 20720, USA.
May 15, 2023.

Introduction

In my search for a spiritual way, I read books, including scriptures. I listened to the religious sermons and conversed with people from all walks of life. When that did not suffice, I travelled around the world, meeting people and experiencing cultures, past and present. All this has enriched my life for which I am mighty glad; and it has brought me to a way of living which I do not hesitate to call a spiritual way.

This journey of my life has brought me freedom in the inner and outer aspects of my life. It has brought me happiness, sometimes even ecstasy. The two together have filled my world with sweet peace of fulfilling harmony within my inner self as well as around me in my external world.

When Buddha found enlightenment, he did not just live happily within his Nirvana ever after the enlightenment; rather, he wanted to bring others to discover and experience Nirvana and enlightenment. This seems to be an essential aspect of the spiritual way of living. There is a compelling instinct towards sharing, as if the enlightenment and Nirvana remain unfulfilled and unfulfilling without this sharing.

This innate urge to share is totally compelling, overpowering, and also guiding towards deeper and deeper enlightenment with more and more enriching encounters with Nirvana. The spiritual way is a life-long journey of experimentation, observation, and the experiential lessons that evolve because we "witness" life in all its colors – deep within ourselves as well as out in the near and far horizons. I have "witnessed" some of the wonders. The inner urge compels me to spread the gospel of "spiritual way" so that all can do the same, of course in their own way.

Under this inner urging, I have continued my journey even after I had found and experienced my spiritual way. There is an innate reason for that: I call this reason by the name "equivalence principle" which seems to operate universally. It is the principle that harmonizes and unifies our inner and spiritual life with our mundane living in the outer world, both locally and globally.

In 2011, I started work on formally encompassing the "spiritual way" via a theory of spirituality. It is now 2023 and the book has not been published yet. And when it does get published, I have a strong feeling that it will try to talk about what can only be "witnessed" and cannot be talked about.

During this long period, I have done many experimentations. These have tested the theory in many specific situations in my life. I have also traveled around the globe and consulted many people on the globetrotting trails. These have included university professors, students, professionals, and backpackers. The theory of spirituality, in its current form, has withstood the tests of these experimentations and observations. In turn, the experimentation and validation processes have helped with a more encompassing expression of the theory.

This book gives some insight into the process, and shares with the readers some unusual circumstances and efforts that I have incorporated in formulating this spiritual way of living life. These observations and experiments have involved thoughts and situations. Some directly focus on aspects of the theory, and some are thoughts that I have entertained while traveling, walking and hiking.

While exploring the "spiritual way", I have tried to lift some constraints in an effort to leave the scope of the exploration wide open, and not to narrowly focus on what I regard as spirituality, or is traditionally so regarded. If we focus too narrowly on what our preconceived notions and concepts are, then we are apt to miss what is important but outside the narrow scope of the search within our concepts.

This book presents my pursuit in four different pathways. It starts with a series of "discourses" on subjects that directly surround the "spiritual way". The subjects include spiritual notions; meaning of life; happiness, fulfillment, and peace; human feelings, passions, and pursuits; Sufi notions of travel and journeying; and the basic notions of a happy and fulfilled life with peace within and peace around.

These discourses present most of the elements necessary for a "spiritual way" for living, without detailing the "way" itself. That will be the subject of a subsequent book. However, an inquisitive reader may formulate a way on one's own because the necessary building blocks are already here.

Next section deals with the phenomenon of "witnessing". It is something that happens, it just happens without any exercise in analytics or synthetics. Mostly, it happens when we are just there, we are just present – not seeking or searching. We are just peacefully there. When it does happen, it can lay our life bare in front of us, all our life from "a" to "z" regarding a particular matter. Every aspect that we are concerned about is demonstrated to us to our entire satisfaction, and every question that occurs to us is answered fully without holding anything back. This "witnessing" phenomenon is completely different, but consistent with in its results, from the processes of "scientific observation" which are analytical and synthetical in their nature. The "witnessing" happens instantaneously without any role for analytics and synthetics. Therefore, no matter one's formal qualifications, anyone and everyone can "witness" – the results are enlightening, as was the case with Buddha.

While traveling and journeying helped me mainly at the level of "scientific observations", what I sought was to witness my 'self'. Some say it can happen through meditation. It happened to me, without any explicit intent or planning, but instantaneously, because of circumstances that occurred but I had not sought them out. Such witnessing can leave its marks deep within our inner self, marks that are ineffable though very concretely present. This is the subject matter of the section on "witnessing experiments". These experiments also serve for verification and validation of the elements of the "way" that I have expressed in my discourses.

I have further elaborated these elements in the third section of the book, where I have shared some observations that occurred to me while walking, hiking, or after meditating. These observations elaborate and add to the elements of the "way" that are in my discourses.

There is a part of our lives that we spend while sleeping. Often, we experience dreams and nightmares. Most we do not remember upon waking up, or they fizzle away soon after. There are some intense ones that persist somewhat longer. Their significance, if any, for the "way" of living is not clear, though their presence is a fact of life. I have documented few such occurrences in my own life. They have played no role in the formulation of the "way" and are documented in Appendix A, just as examples without a directional intent.

This "spiritual way" has set me free from wants and free from fear. It has guided me through thick and thin with wonderful smoothness, almost with elatedness. It has shown me glimpses of richness in poverty, and glimpses of poverty in richness, and made my heart exalt with the abundance that abounds all around.

This spiritual way is wide open for everyone, as will be seen while reading the detailed descriptions. The word "spiritual" refers to an inward-looking view in the sense of self-discovery. By no means it requires us to be religious or even godly. If we are religious, the spiritual way is wide open for us; and if we are not religious, the spiritual way is wide open for us. If we believe in god, the spiritual way is wide open for us; and if we do not believe in god, the spiritual way is wide open for us. The spiritual way is for all humans. It works for all humans irrespective of their religiosity. It works for all humans whether they are theist, atheist, agnostic, or gnostic. In this approach, spirituality exists independently in its own right, not as an addendum to religion. We call it spiritual though there are no spirits in it. This spiritual way is totally immanent, with no mystic or transcendental elements to it. From the bottom of my heart and the top of the world where I live, I invite everyone to share this freedom and abundance with me.

Discourses

Pursuit of Happiness

I was thinking, just thinking[1]. There were many thoughts, a train of thoughts, some related some unrelated. I cannot recall them, but perhaps one. I thought about what I was doing, and what I wanted to do. It was induced by a query from my son. He said he realizes what we must have gone through in bringing him and his siblings up, and that now it was their turn to make us happy. So, he asked "what would make you happy?"

I realized that I was doing things with very modest expectations and aspirations. My idea of happiness was simply to avoid being unhappy. I did not want to feel insulted and brutalized; that was happiness to me. But I had never asked myself what would make me happy, really happy! My son put that thought in my mind, for the first time in my life!

All throughout my life I was unconsciously driven towards being something like some role models. So, I wanted to be a thinker, a scholar, a famous leader, or an epitome of a scientific discoverer. But to be happy, fulfilled, and at peace? The thought was never raised in my mind as something to become.

---

[1] Bowie, Md: Sunday April 2nd, 2017.

In the course of life some of my role models stopped being my heroes. I still admired them but not desired to become like them. So, for a while I just floated without a direction that would attract me. I was not lost; I was seeking. I still wanted to become something like those old role models. That is because the original goals perhaps did not go away with me losing reverence for my heroes that originally inspired the goals.

I had lost respect for my heroes because when I scrutinized their lives and their accomplishments, I discovered that as human beings they were not as transparent, and the society had elevated their accomplishments to raise them to become much larger than life.

And then there was religion. It had imbued in me a fear and uncertainty due to intangible religious concepts and teachings. I did not like acting out of fear. I wanted something positive to motivate me.

So, I tried to change my outlook towards religion. I wanted to take fear out of it. I tried to remove concepts and practices that made one psychologically unsure, dependent and weak. Further, I started rejecting concepts and practices that divided humanity.

I continued on to take fear out of religion. I liberated myself from this fear and stopped those practices that were suggested using the fear factor. I knew conscientiously that the fear was unfounded. I went beyond the conscientious level and developed an axiomatic scientific approach to realize that the fear factor was unfounded.

I looked around the world. I saw people who had liberated themselves from such fear factors, and had achieved happiness. This happiness came from being liberated and gave them a mysterious grace and a generous heart. They had found happiness even under cruel circumstances, even while being suppressed and oppressed.

I had done all this without explicitly asking the question: what would make me happy! Such questions are often times shelved in favor of others that we are trained to deem of a higher precedence.

The pursuit of happiness had not been the motivating factor. The deriving force had so far been a need to liberate from the fear factor and the societal and religious exploitation founded on it.

For the first time in my life, because of the prodding by my son, I asked myself: what would make me happy? I pondered over this question. The answer was this: I wanted to do what my heart desires, and that would make me happy.

That brings in the question of laws ad constraints that might apply to me while pursuing my heart's desire towards my happiness.

Do I mean that there are no constraints or laws that I need to observe? This obviously cannot be so. For, on one hand there is the law of hunger that requires that I must eat; that implies that I must earn my food and shelter and clothes – I must subsist. So, I can do my heart's desire to the extent that I can also accept the constraints on my activities needed to secure subsistence.

There is another aspect. If the existence of laws makes my happiness less likely, then there is an opposition between laws and happiness. Some laws exist for the sake of happiness; such is the law of hunger, the law of health, and the law of life itself such as breathing.

Without these laws, life or health would not be possible and happiness requires life and health.

Now my happiness is for me to do what my heart desires. There are obvious limitations to it imposed by the laws that apply to the processes of life and health. These limitations must be accepted as the limiting factors to my happiness. Therefore, there can exist no absolute happiness without limitations, even if some of these limitations are prerequisites for happiness itself to exist.

The question then arises, what kind of limitations do I accept and what kind of limitations do I reject?

How do I know which limitations I must accept? I guess only experimentation can tell. I can start with full absolute happiness without limitations, and discover limitations one by one, and accept each limitation or fight it out.

The process is an experimentation. For example, in the process of an experiment I may discover that I need to accept a limitation, and later on the experimentation may demonstrate that such acceptance is unnecessary or even harmful for the pursuit of my happiness. I would then decide to reject the limitation that I had earlier accepted. Likewise, I may reject a limitation and subsequently discover that it is actually beneficial for my happiness. Pursuit of happiness is, therefore, a continued effort with experimentation. It takes place in a free flow manner.

Rejection of a limitation means fighting out the restrictions that it apparently imposes on my ability to pursue happiness. Rejecting a limitation does not imply its invalidation; it just means that I will not allow it to limit my happiness as I currently understand the situation.

An existing law may operate without imposing restrictions on my freedom to pursue what my heart desires and thus to achieve happiness. For instance, the laws that lead the flowers to bloom may impose no restrictions on my happiness; on the other hand, they may enhance my happiness. Similarly, the law of hunger is to enhance my happiness because without eating I will not have the health and consciousness to be happy. The situation is such that the laws exist: some enhance my happiness and some restrict my happiness.

Take the law of hunger. It is established that without eating I cannot pursue my heart's desire and thus be happy; in fact, nobody can be happy without food. For a rich person this law imposes no restriction on his happiness; while for a destitute, this law can deny him happiness altogether by demanding all his time and resources merely to acquire subsistence.

Nature has not created situations whereby a person is so destitute that he cannot pursue happiness. Therefore, an optimal chance to pursue happiness is to act according to one's *natural* conscience, which roughly translates into following one's heart. However, society can produce situations that can render a person so destitute that he cannot pursue happiness. Such situations are created during famine, war and abject poverty. So, it can be generally postulated that situations or laws that make a person so destitute as to cause him to completely fail in the

13

pursuit of happiness – such situations and laws are not *natural* and may be rejected.

One might wonder about the kind of things that my heart might desire. This depends on my world-view: which represents the way I view the world. It also represents what happiness means to me. For the present, one may use the term "spiritual way" to represent what my heart might desire in the pursuit of my happiness. This way of looking at a spiritual way is new, simple, natural and fresh. It can, however, be disruptive of its view that a religion might advocate invoking the fear factor.

Let us explore a simple consequence of this view of a spiritual way. Consider the law of health. It implies that my happiness will depend upon my physical state. My state of health determines my ability to think and feel, which in turn determine what my heart desires. Thoughts and feelings are, therefore, spiritual instruments. These determine what my heart desires, and also help fulfill it. In other words, they determine what happiness means to me, and they help to actually realize it. This illustrates a coupling between the physical health and the spiritual instruments of thoughts and feelings. Such a coupling is a manifestation of a general principle that I call "equivalence principle". It establishes spirituality in physicality, and physicality in spirituality.

Likewise, the state of poverty can limit my ability to pursue my heart's desire, and thus my ability to achieve happiness. The resources at my disposal are, therefore, a limiting factor for me to pursue my happiness. These resources determine how I deal with the applicable laws, meaning reject or accept each law. The laws that control the resources are the determinants of the landscape within which all people can acquire happiness.

Again, nature has not created any laws that deprive a person of the resources to such an extent that he or she cannot pursue happiness. Society, on the other hand can create laws that lead to abject poverty which prohibits pursuit of happiness. Such situations are not *natural* and they can be rejected because they stand in the people's pursuit of happiness.

My spirituality represents "what my heart desires" and therefore my happiness. The extant that I can pursue my desires, is subject to my health, the resources that I can muster and my state of poverty or richness. The three factors, together, determine how happy I can be. The most important factor is the state of my spirituality because it represents my desires, and thus my happiness. An advanced spiritual state represents such desires that most laws will not impose limitations on fulfilling them. Then happiness is maximally achievable, largely independent of the resources. This is what Sufis and Saints do.

I have actually been pursuing my happiness most of my life, even if I did not explicitly explore the dynamics of my happiness until recently, when my son prodded me about it. It became easier after retirement because then the work-related constraints were eliminated. I have the material resources that I do, and I discover that they are adequate for me to pursue my happiness. I asked myself: would the pursuit of my happiness be different if I had more material resources? Offhand I think the answer is no. Having said that, I must assert that one of my heart's desires is to help fellow human beings and to bring about positive change in the world. Limitation of material resources does limit my ability to do that. This brings forth the question: are all the desires of my heart equally significant for my happiness? Again, my spiritual maturity plays a crucial role in answering such questions.

Different persons will wish to undertake different activities in the pursuit of their happiness. Each person needs to have a heart-to-heart conversation with themselves in exploring what happiness means to them, and what activities they want to undertake in the pursuit of their happiness. One of the things that I have done in the pursuit of my happiness is to travel worldwide. This has provided a much wider scope to know the meanings of my happiness. It has opened my world-view with respect to how different societies view life, how different countries manifest their culture and civilization, and how different cultures and civilizations treat fundamental human values in terms of respect for the individual, non-discriminatory behavior, just and equitable policies for the sharing of resources, and opportunities for the pursuit of one's happiness. Such travels have helped me to become wiser through making my spirituality more mature.

It must be realized that my family and friends also impact the pursuit of my happiness. Lives are intertwined, so that happiness cannot be achieved without helpful cooperation with the family and friends. Here, again, the spiritual maturity plays a critical role, because it determines how my happiness depends upon the actions and choices that members of my family and friends make with respect to the entanglement of their lives with mine. If I am spiritually mature, I will handle the nature of this entanglement wisely. It soon becomes clear that pursuit of my happiness is vitally intertwined with the happiness of others; and sharing practices among the people become an important aspect of the maturity of one's spirituality.

Happiness is a journey, not a destination, and journeys have intended or unintended detours. A journey can even change its destination because of a better understanding of and experiments with happiness. It is all up to the heart.

Purpose and Meaning of Life

I am doing some activism, some writing, some development for a technology platform, and some Physics and IT research[2].

The things that I am doing, why am I doing them?

Am I doing these things to make a difference in the world? Not explicitly so. I am doing what I am doing in pursuit of my happiness. It seems it does not matter what I am doing as long as I feel happy and fulfilled doing it. My purpose is to pursue my happiness.

So, what is the purpose of my life to start with? What is the meaning of my life? It appears that life is reflexive. It directs such queries to itself. So, the meaning of life is life itself. Whatever I do in pursuit of my happiness, to keep myself happy and fulfilled, that is exactly the meaning of my life. The purpose of my life is exactly to do those things in pursuit of my happiness.

So, what was all that gibberish that we were taught: to live a meaningful life, and the purpose of life being to rise up to reach God? That gibberish was to streamline our mind so we do not rock the boat that other people owned and enjoyed, and they had decided that we were there just to row it for their pleasure!

---

[2] Bowie, Md. Sunday, April 9th, 2017.

19

It is ironic that I should have spent all my life more or less rowing that boat for other people. That is before I realized this simple truth – the truth that the purpose of my life was to pursue my happiness, and the meaningful life was to engage in activities that help me pursue my happiness! The truth was always simple. But those people, the clergy and the ruling class, had trivialized this truth for its simplicity and naturalness. They ridiculed it and bad mouthed it. They transformed and decorated their deceit and selfishness with holy ideas and glamor to place it on a pedestal, and they presented it as the purpose for me to aspire for.

When there were only six people in the world, there was one Kane amongst them. They hide by their allotropies. People who we suspect, like the religious clergy and the self-serving rich, they are also entangled into the web like everyone else is. It seems it is the devil himself, having morphed himself as the Divine. The devil has made himself into Divine, and he misleads us when we look for answers in the exterior world. The only source of Truth is within our own "self". We can trust only our own self. Everything else is potentially from the devil.

*

I thought about what is the purpose of life[3]. I felt the purpose of life is simply to live it happily. Any other purpose will require value judgment. Even altruism as a purpose is value judgment because it thinks serving others selflessly is somehow a desired goal, pretending

---

[3] Bowie, MD: Wednesday, May 02, 2018.

that it leads to happiness or transcendence! The purpose of human life is not drastically different from a purpose to animal life. It is a pretense, perhaps coming from scriptures, that man was created special, a vice regent of God. Putting a different purpose for human life translates into a value judgment, using an arbitrarily chosen value system.

So, my take was that the purpose of life is solely to live it happily in a way that the person finds fulfilling at any given time. What is happy and fulfilling will change with time, and it will be personal. Each person defines what happiness and fulfillment means to him or her, without any external imposition in that regard.

I thought that a life lived in this way is a journey which is not a continuous travel but a travel between a discrete set of "destinations". At any given time, a person has an idea of where his fulfillment lies and he strives to get there. However, as soon as he gets there, he soon finds that his fulfillment is someplace else, and, therefore, he starts to travel towards this new destination. Thus, a person is a perpetual traveler, moving from one fulfillment destination to another.

Life begins to decay if it stops being in this perpetual motion; of travel from one fulfillment destination to the next. In this decay state the fulfillment of the person also begins to decay. This begins another sequence of travels, this time not selected by the person, but imposed by the process of decay. The decay process sets in for one reason: the person feels too insecure and becomes fearful. It is the feeling of insecurity and fear that if he continues to travel towards the next destination, he might not make it and lose what he has already acquired in the process. This is because leaving one fulfillment destination for another always includes two things: risk of loss of the current fulfillment level, and acquisition of a greater fulfillment level. As one lives on, a person becomes less certain of his capabilities because of aging and consequent loss of 'marketability' in the society. He becomes more fearful of not being able to make up to the next destination level; and he becomes less hopeful and keen and ecstatic about what the next fulfillment destination has to offer.

When this decay state arrives, the journey does not stop. Rather, it continues along a retrograde trajectory of diminishing fulfillment. This eventually leads to death, when the travel actually ends. One reaches the point of death in two senses. First, the decay process eats into the fulfillment of the person and the person succumbs due to unhappiness. Further, the decay process of diminishing fulfillment and resultant succumbing to increasing unhappiness, causes a biological decay which has to lead to a point of death. The two aspects of the decay leading to death are very intertwined and, in some sense, causally linked, such that they mutually reinforce each other.

The journey before this decay process also had the two aspects: the excitement of reaching the next fulfillment destination brought forth hope and ecstasy which also resulted in biological growth and strength.

Life is thus a continuous travel, towards a specific destination at any given time. The destinations change over time. The travel between these destinations brings greater hope and ecstasy which in turn also brings strength and growth in biological terms. When a person decides not to travel to a next destination, the journey still continues, but now with reduced hope and ecstasy and resultant biological weakening and decay. Life never stops journeying; either we decide the trajectory of travel or the decay process will set in and determine this trajectory for us.

*

It is all relative as well as transient[4]. There being no absolute reality or truth. The truth within our "self", the truth within their selves, and the truth within my self – they are all truth and they represent different manifestation of "happiness". I hold it as self-evident that everyone has a right to the pursuit of happiness. So, let the river of life flow for every-one's life in pursuit of happiness. That is the purpose and meaning of every life.

The sole meaning of my life is to be respectful towards the desires in my heart and also to the desires in other hearts; the sole purpose of my life is to follow my heart in pursuit of my happiness while letting others pursue their happiness. It is to be happy, without being greedy, and to be together with everyone else because we are all in pursuit of happiness, and together we can do it better.

That means that the meaning and purpose of life is to live it happily and to live it conscientiously. This is the only truth.

Questions like a creator of the universe are not natural questions that would occur to a person; rather, they are planted externally by the high priests of the religion and the rulers of a society in collusion. The

---

[4] Bowie, MD: November 6th, 2020.

23

priests and rulers have traditionally been in collusion on these topics. The collusion enables them to have their pleasure rides in their boats, and to be able to educate us on behalf of this creator so that we will consider it a privilege to row these boats for them.

To really dwell on my meaning and my purpose, I might look within my "self", listen to my own "self", and then see if it leads to something like a transcendental being or to some absolute looking truth. I actually did this experiment diligently. I did find some transcendental entity but it was nothing like the Creator God that the religions present to us. Such an entity that I found makes no demands of us like the religions do; it loves us unconditionally, and it keeps our wellbeing and happiness in the fore front. It is more like a parent-infant relationship that this transcendental entity has with us. It represents total benevolence and compassion, and it is entirely nonjudgmental.

I can explore further and ask questions like what are my inherent needs and my inherent capabilities. It is not unlikely that my heart desires to fulfill what my needs are, and it is highly plausible that my happiness lies in being able to fulfill those needs. I did this enquiry as well, and I found that our capabilities are there to serve our needs. There is no need that is left unserved, and there is no unneeded capability.

Human needs fall progressively in four categories. First come the survival needs. These are our needs for air, water, food, and shelter. All persons require them for the continuation of individual life. Second are the sexual needs. These are planted within all persons to ensure continuation of the species. Third is the need to upbring the children.

This seems to be less of a universal need because some people abandon their children. It is not clear if this need is inherent to a person, or does a person do it as an obligation to society, religion, and legal considerations. Does a person do it as a result of his love for the child, this love being inherently present? More data is needed to understand this issue. But looking at animals it seems as though upbringing the children is part of a person for the perpetuation of the species. If so, it could be an auxiliary need that arises to complement the sexual need. Fourth is the sharing need: this means the need to interact with other people, offer them what we have, and receive from them what they have. It is done at parity level between the giver and the receiver because the receiver in one instance becomes the giver in another. It is not done in a spirit of barter; rather, it is done in a spirit of togetherness. Sometimes it is called a social need; however, social interaction often does not include sharing in the above sense, and it often includes things like social recognition, fame, and richness which are not included in the spirit of sharing and togetherness. Sharing practices represent a relationship of togetherness between the practitioners of sharing. It is not to be confused with trade which often is motivated by profit and sometimes greed. It also is not to be confused with religious charity which falls so short of the sharing with togetherness, because it has an upper hand that gives and a lower hand that receives, thus violating the parity requirement.

The above four needs are mostly adequate for living a happy, fulfilling, and peaceful life. The first three needs are rather biological in nature. The fourth is psychological or spiritual depending upon how we perceive it and how we practice it.

It is sometimes the case that the above four needs do not satisfy an individual. For example, some passions, aspirations, and feelings may remain unaddressed. To achieve these, we need an in depth understanding of ourselves and the life within us and the life around us. This understanding, rather "witnessing", generates wisdom.

With wisdom it is possible to satisfy the above four needs such that the unfulfilled feelings and passions can be realized as well. This could be regarded as the 5th need. We can call it the need for self-discovery to "know" ourselves, which is another name for an in depth understanding of ourselves and our environment. It can be regarded as our "spiritual way". Our spiritual way is our 5th need which is inherently associated with the pursuit of happiness: to know happiness and to know the ways to pursue it. In other words, we fulfill the first four needs and we do it in such a way that is in accord with our fifth need. In yet other words, we meet the first four needs wisely. Wisdom and the spiritual way are one and the same thing.

There are no human needs other than these five.

Now we might ask, what are the capabilities that we innately possess to meet these needs? There are three capabilities: our senses, our intellect, and our conscience. These are innate to man and they are adequate to meet all the human needs. The first two capabilities enable the first three needs. The last two needs, namely the sharing and self-discovery, require conscience as well as intellect and senses.

In our discussion no need arose to have a discourse on questions like "the purpose of life" or "who is the creator" or "who am I" or "why am I here" or "what am I" or "what will happen to me after death". Such topics are superfluous because they do not occur to people naturally; rather, they are planted into our heads by priests and rulers acting in collusion, so that they can align us along their goals.

So, is there life after death? We have dismissed these questions as planted question, because they do not arise naturally to a person. Have we avoided confronting such questions? No, there has been no evasion of genuine enquiry. We have not addressed them because they did not occur to us, except via the priests and rulers trying to artificially plant them into our enquiry. The devil will try to use doubt. What if the questions are genuine? That doubt induces fear, and fear is man's worst enemy. I would not entertain something motivated by doubt and fear. These are instruments of exploitation, and have been used to exploit us since time immemorial. The universe is "reasonable" as we observe it, and it will respect our need to be ourselves and free from fear.

Seekers of the Spiritual Way

Just as you go to places and observe whatever happens to be there, you go to spiritual places and observe whatever happens to be there[5].

Where are the spiritual places? Every place is a spiritual place if you are in a spiritual state while there. When are you in your spiritual state? You are in a spiritual state when you are looking inside yourself. When are you looking inside yourself? You are looking inside yourself when you are talking to your inner self; when you are thinking about things that concern your inner self; when you are asking questions that concern your inner self. You decide what concerns your inner self, and that becomes part of your spirituality.

Spirituality eventually expresses itself in physical things, physical actions and physical events. For example, spirituality expresses itself in sharing. Love expresses itself also in sharing, in being together, in sharing yourself with the other.

What happens after you have made a discovery? Historical examples show that you come to share it with other people! May be that is because sharing is a deeply spiritual thing; or may be sharing is inherent to man because of his togetherness attribute with others. Sharing is an example of a spiritual activity when you do it out of love;

---

[5] Bowie, MD: Monday Sept 8, 2014.

in other words, when you do it altruistically and obliviously, as your primary nature.

An important way to observe spirituality is to observe it in other people. See what they regard as spiritual. See how they go about expressing it. See how they go about achieving it.

Spirituality must express itself in physical things because of the "law of shadows" and because of "equivalence principle". These imply that everything spiritual has a physical manifestation, and everything physical has a spiritual manifestation. Therefore, there is not a sharp division between what is spiritual and what is physical. Much depends on the thinking behind the physical action, and the intent behind the action. For example, a man walking his dog, is it a spiritual thing, is it a physical thing? It can be either depending upon the thinking or intent of the man walking his dog. If he walked his dog as a mere habit, as a needed action which is part of his routine, and it is not related to any matter connected to his inner self - then it is a physical act. If he is walking his dog because of his love for the dog, or because it brings him inner happiness - then it is a spiritual act. If both kind of motivations exist, for example it is his neighbor's dog that he is pet-sitting for money, but it also brings him inner happiness because of his love for dogs - then it is both a physical act as well as a spiritual act.

You observe your inner self and you find out spirituality. You find out spirituality just as you find out physicality. You discover the spiritual world, and no matter how far you discover it, you never exhaust it; just as you research physical world and you never exhaust it. The discoveries continue infinitely in both worlds.

Both type of discoveries use the same methods. They both use processes like "observing", "learning", "analyzing", and "theorizing".

I am both a scientist and a seeker of spirituality. As a scientist I use observing, learning, analyzing, and theorizing; but in science I use only these processes with nothing else (like "internalizing" and "witnessing") added to these processes. In science, I use them not as a single unitary process but as separate processes to be combined latter. I need to learn these processes as fields of scientific specialization needing substantial training.

As a seeker of spirituality, I need no such specialized training. Life is for everyone to live. However, observation, learning, analysis, and theorization nevertheless take place in the process of living. These happen almost unconsciously as parts of the processes of life. Ironically, specialized training often is so focused on specializations that it can be an obstacle in learning a wholistic picture which is the focus in spiritual seeking.

In addition to observation, learning, analysis, and theorization, there are two other processes that play a vital role for a seeker of spirituality. These are "internalization" and "witnessing": processes that are not used by scientists but are special to seeking spirituality.

Like other processes, internalization also happens automatically in the process of living. No conscious effort is needed. If you get burned in a flame, you know not to go into the flame again and not to get burned again. That is internalization of knowledge about burning. If you love

31

the ecstasy that you experienced, you know that you want to have more of it. That is internalization of the knowledge about ecstasy. It happens automatically. However, internalization is more than this, and this is where a seeker of spirituality begins to depart from the ways of the scientist. The seeker makes a solemn commitment: he or she will save himself from burning and, just as much, also save others from burning; he or she will enjoy ecstasy and share this knowledge about ecstasy with others. In a nutshell, because of such solemn commitment, the seeker of spirituality lives not as an individual but as part of a universal humanity. In other words, the seeker lives in togetherness with others.

As a seeker of spirituality, I am required to practice sharing in a sincerely committed way. Difficulty for the spiritual seeker enters at this stage. The monkey wrench comes in when I try to share! It comes in when I try to commit myself to share honestly and sincerely. Will I protect others from getting burned by the flame, knowing that the flame does burn? Will I actually burn others in the flame so that I do not have to compete with them? Will I honestly share my knowledge about ecstasy with others, after having enjoyed the ecstatic experience? Will I actually keep my knowledge as a secret, so others will not have it because I fear others will have it at my expense? Difficulties arise because of the spiritual requirement that I sincerely commit to the welfare of others as I commit to my own welfare. It is extremely trying to keep this commitment, because greed is around and tempting.

My hypothesis is this. Our natural inclination is to protect others from getting burnt. Our natural inclination is to share our knowledge about ecstasy with others. The behavior to the contrary is a learned behavior from the indoctrinations that we are subjected to. This indoctrination teaches us greed. The greed teaches us evil acts: so, contrary to our natural instincts, we decide to burn others; and contrary to our innate sharing instinct, we keep our experience of ecstasy a secret and refuse to share it. Underlying both, the evil and the selfishness, is just one thing and that is greed.

Is greed within us? Are we greedy by birth? My hypothesis is that greed is not innate. Greed is acquired. Ironically it is acquired through a process of observation, learning, analysis, and theorization! It arises out of rational processes. Therefore, science is a double-edged thing: it helps us understand and it also helps us to misuse our understanding. One reason for this mixed result is that science is not wholistic: in fact, it leaves out most of the aesthetics in the processes of living our lives.

On the contrary, as a seeker of spirituality I take a wholistic view of life. I am intrinsically removed from the tendency to acquire knowledge and then to misuse it. The tendency to misuse knowledge comes strictly from a non-wholistic and partial approach to life that lacks commitment and partitions the unitary whole into artificial and rather devilish partition of the whole into "us" versus "them".

Is observation, learning, analysis, and theorization something that leads you to greed and subsequently to evil and selfishness? It obviously can because man does do evil and does become selfish. Then there are also Sufis, saints and prophets who are not evil and they do not act selfish.

As noted earlier, there are two elements, namely internalization and witnessing, that differentiate between a scientific approach and the approach of a seeker of spirituality. Answer to the above puzzle can lie in these two elements. These elements lead to a view of life that goes beyond knowledge into the "internalization and sharing" of the knowledge, which totally commits to a sincere welfare of all.

I share an experiment that I conducted. It just happened while I was meditating, expecting nothing but making an attempt at seeking my inward view. I asked of myself if there is something within me and what its response will be if I called it?

Then I looked within me. I found nothing other than the internal organs of the body. I recognized those as not me. So, what was me? What it was that I call my inner self, that I call my spirituality?

At that moment, it felt as if all that talk about the inner self was nothing, just a void! There was a void within me and there was a similar void outside of me: the two voids were the same and they were connected. The universe was just a void. The void had no structure, no illumination, no darkness. But it felt peaceful: not happy or fulfilling, just peaceful. For a short while I sat there, rather happily contented and satisfied, not perturbed by things that were there. Not concerned about things that were not going well; not feeling anxious to set anything right, or to get anything done.

Perhaps I had a small encounter with "silence" and "stillness". In that state, the words and actions were not forbidden, but they did not seem needed, or there seemed to exist no place that called for them. The universe was perfect as it was!

Disconnection

I thought about the "analytic" approach used by the scientists and "witnessing" approach used by the seekers of spirituality, how they produce such different results[6].

I did an experiment: how would it be if an action is disconnected from its intended result? To disconnect an effort from its outcome, like it happens when we turn the sound off in a music video. The actions and motions that the singers and musicians do, they make sense to us through the sound that they produce. Without the sound the efforts are disconnected from the outcome of the effort. And this disconnection makes the effort lose its meaning.

Something similar happens when we replace the spiritual approach with scientific approach.

That disconnection happens a lot in our daily lives. For example, the connection between a job that we do and the food that we have on our table. There is obviously a connection because without a source of income we would not be able to buy the food. However, an explicit connection between a particular job and the particular food items on the table is allusive. This connection is often so long and winding that it is a disconnection in practical and operational terms. Therefore, the work

---

[6] Bowie, MD: March 25th, 2021.

done on the job often becomes meaningless, like the actions of the singer in the absence of the song. This disconnection creates confusion and disappointment, sabotaging our pursuit for happiness. While any job will put food on the table, only some jobs will enhance our happiness.

The set of values that a person has is the thing that makes this connection or not! That is because the set of our values is our spirituality; it gives us our world-view. It is through the value system that a connection gets made between the effort and its outcome.

If there is a disconnect between my set of values and that of the others, then others will not see the connection between my efforts and the outcome as I will see it; and some will see the opposite of what I will see. The values of one society are different from those of another. That is because their lives are different, and they have witnessed different things in their history and culture. Consequently, their happiness means different things for each, and they take different paths for the pursuit of their happiness.

Disconnection happens when the wholistic unitarity is replaced with dualities, partitions and segmentations: when things that really go together are artificially separated apart.

Unified Existence: One Existence

Let us do an experiment[7]. The equivalence principle asserts that there are physical manifestations of spiritual happenings, and vice versa. There is an equivalence between the spiritual and the physical. The duality between them is only perceptual. Consider a unification of physical and spiritual worlds. If there is a unified existence, what is this unified existence? Is the unified existence simply the sum of the two worlds? Will its manifestations continue to be the usual things as we know them now? Will there be a river, a mountain, a man, an animal, and a forest in the unified existence?

It seems that all existence is just an appearance of some reality. That means the rivers, mountains, man, lion, and tree do not exist except in the sense of a projection of the reality. These things seem to exist as a projection in terms of a physics-model that uses the space-time constructs. The physicists do not really know what time is, nor do they know what space is. There is, therefore, nothing sacrosanct in a physics-model that uses the space-time constructs.

Consider a new physics-model in which the space-time is eliminated. Such a model is possibly worthwhile because the space and time are not well understood in science. Let us employ some new

---

[7] Bowie, MD: Monday Sept 8, 2014. and March 25th, 2021.

constructs, like the "commitment" and "witnessing" constructs that I have described earlier. What would be the shape of things in the new physics, modeled using the commitment and witnessing constructs?

If there is to be a unified existence as we have talked about, will it remain unaltered in the new physics model? Will it remain invariant under the change of the physics constructs? Or will it change with the physics constructs and behave like a projection of some new reality?

Let us give this unified existence a name, let us call it "One Existence". Is this One Existence a projection that changes with the change in the model constructs of physics, or does it remain invariant under such changes? If it remains invariant then it potentially behaves like an absolute reality that exists by itself, and it is not just a projection of some other reality? If the unified existence, or One Existence, is absolute reality, rather than a projection of some other reality, can we derive some of its attributes? Attributes are important because they help us know this One Existence. If One Existence attributes cannot be derived, in that case we cannot know it; One Existence may exist in that situation, but it will not be relevant in our lives.

For example, we cannot derive the attributes of One Existence from the attributes of man. That is because in such an approach One Existence cannot represent an absolute reality, as it would strongly depend on the assumption that One Existence Attributes can be derived from the known attributes of man – if man is not an absolute reality, the attributes of man can change, and therefore One Existence would need to change and it would then not be an absolute reality. In such a scenario

One Existence Attributes would be a model dependent projection, contradicting the ansatz that One Existence is absolute.

If such contradiction appears in all attempts at constructing One Existence Attributes, then it would show that the One Existence is not absolute but a model dependent projection. That is likely the case because everything else that we know is a projection and nothing is an absolute reality.

Religions bypass such scrutiny by insisting on blind faith and forbidding such an enquiry.

Man is Innately Good

One of the basic aspects of my theory of spirituality is that man is innately good, and he acts bad only under the influence of indoctrination by the society[8]. The society consists of other people that he interacts with, the religion he confesses, the government he lives under, and global environment that affect his living conditions.

As I travel, I keep an eye to know the life of the people and their cultural and traditional values. I met a French couple who were traveling together through Sarajevo. The hostel was cheap and I stayed a week there; I guess they were doing the same. As I talked about my theory of spirituality, he said he had met a girl who was into astrology, and she had told him that he will soon meet his guru. His girlfriend clarified that I was the guru he was meant to meet.

At first, I thought he was disagreeing with my basic point that our inside (our spirituality) knows the best about what is good and what is bad for us; and I spun my wheels trying to establish this basic point. But he was in fact in agreement on this and other points of the theory, and was rather pleased that we had that conversation.

But really, is this point valid? I felt that this question needs to be revisited and reestablished.

---

[8] Sarajevo: May 12th, 2015.

Machiavelli argues that all valid truths will not combine into a single truth; rather, they will combine and give rise to conflicting truths that cannot be reconciled on rational basis. That is why contest and war happen. The paradigm of the survival of the fittest, or the powerful decide the truth, arises from that conflict and war.

My premise for assuming innately good nature for humans is based on my personal experience over long years, my worldwide travels, and my observation of the behavior of children worldwide. The children help each other, play with each other, and enjoy each other; and they also snatch each other's toys, they byte each other, and they hit each other. They have no discrimination like color, appearance, and language. They also hold no malice; children fighting one instance can be playing together another.

Do such observations support an innately good nature for human beings? Does a person have both good and evil in him from the start? The question is important for spiritual seekers. If a person is born with a good nature and evil is acquired, the task is relatively easier because he only has to shed the external indoctrination that can lead to evil. On the other hand, if a person is born with good and evil both, then the task of the spiritual seeker is harder. That is because not only has he to shed the external influences that lead to evil, in addition, he has also to overcome his innate tendency towards evil. If evil exists in man innately, then how can man save himself from this evil?

What happens to my 'inward looking' prescription to a happy peaceful and fulfilled life? It says that man's inner self knows what is best for man; and he can consult his inner self towards a happy, fulfilled, and peaceful living. Is that still possible in the presence of innate evil in man?

The French couple I was discussing it with, dwelled on the corruption of a person's inner-self and thereby misleading the individual towards evil: and I attributed that to the influence of the special interests within a society. I also argued that the corrupted behavior will show its fallacy in due course; then one can shed the corrupted behavior and its sources and causes that come from the society in a stealth way. Therefore, it is always preferable for a person, at any given moment, to trust his own inner self, so that there will be hope of detecting and correcting any mistakes made along the path of seeking.

A Spiritual Theory Can Exist

In Sofia I met an Egyptian guy who had been traveling for 40 years since he was 26. He strongly stated that individual realities will always lead to conflicting realities; and the notion that they will lead to a unified reality is an artificial construct by special interests!

I already stated that truth and reality are just working concepts; there is no ultimate truth or one reality. So why should different working concepts integrate to produce a single coherent concept? In that case why should individual spiritualities give rise to a unified spiritual science?

Let us ask the same questions in the realm of the physical science. The question can be asked of the individual occurrences in the case of the physical world. Individual observers make individual experiments and obtain individual results. We can argue, as has been argued in the spiritual case above, that the individual results can never combine to produce a single coherent result. Why and how should it be that the individual results do actually combine to produce a coherent theory? We do know, for instance, that individual observations of falling objects have given rise to a coherent theory of gravity. Why should individual falling of objects lead to a coherent theory of gravity? Why should there be biological and physical laws?

The existence of underlying operational laws causes the individual results to coherently combine into a valid theory. We hold it a clear possibility that laws operate in the spiritual world as they do in the physical world. These laws will cause the individual spiritual results to coherently combine to produce a valid spiritual theory, just as they do in the case of physical theory.

Motivations, Desires, and Limitations

There are two things: thoughts that occur to a person and the analysis and correlations and filters that the person applies to those thoughts[9]. The outcome of this process is anything but real: call it a momentary reality that finds an abode in the feelings of the person.

I looked at what was happening to me these days. That was my laboratory to reflect on my thoughts, motivations, desires, and limitations. That was a laboratory to examine shifting emotions and actions across conflicting thoughts. For example, I had felt a physical, intellectual, and emotional suffocation. I had felt not respected and not loved. That was suffocating. This thought has been on my mind very actively for over a week now. I asked questions. What is a man? What is he driven by? What are his desires driven by? And what are his limitations?

The night before I had a very unusual dream, rather a nightmare. I saw a boy in my son's home. The boy in the dream was supposed to be his son; he seemed like the same age as his son, however he was fluffier and heavier built, and did not behave like his real son would. This boy would listen to me and not care about what I said, and would show no deference towards me as his grandfather, nor would respond to anything

---

[9] Bowie, MD: Monday, September 11th, 2017.

I would say. This behavior upset me a lot. It woke me up, and could not go back to sleep. I realized I was upset about the behavior of a little boy who did not even exist. The boy was nowhere, and yet he upset me to the extent that I could not sleep! What is the reality of it? The boy is real or unreal? My getting upset is real or unreal? Thinking pragmatically, my getting upset was a very real thing as it deprived me of my sleep and greatly ruffled up my peace, even if the boy causing it was only a mirage! How the real and the unreal permeate into each other in such situations? And most situations in life are such permeations of the real and unreal, with our perception and imagination an integral part of them. We live a mirage!

Pragmatically speaking, it is perhaps expedient to think that for a person his thoughts, his perceptions, his pain, his ecstasy are all real. That is because a person's actions, and consequently the results of his living in this world are determined by such factors. It would appear that everyone lives a 'mirage'! Everyone without an exception! The man in the street, the philosopher, the King, the High Priest – all live a mirage! Me and you and they are all living a mirage!

The actual manifestation of the inbuilt motivation takes place in the gratification of hunger, thirst, protection from the elements, and sex on one hand, and the pursuit of wealth and power on the other. Man in reality pursues his happiness, but ends up pursuing wealth and power confusing them for happiness. And this confusion persists because man seldom takes a pause to consult his own heart in finding where his happiness actually lies.

Consider my impending travel away from home; my going away from home is perhaps a part of the above processes. It is only a single step along the journey; a phase of life among an infinite sequence of phases that are rudely truncated by death.

As I think about going away in three days, it is the beginning of one such phase. I know I will miss home and family. Already I thought to myself I have three more chances to experience this bed of mine. As she snored, first lightly and then heavily, it was not irritating at all; rather, I thought of it as music, real soothing music. See, how my own thoughts and perceptions can change? How my perceptions can change an irritation into musical pleasure? In these shifting sands where is any reality?

Desires are desirable

Just wondering how to have desires but no sadness or pain[10]. The idea seems to be inconsistent with Buddhist thought which seems to imply that desires will lead to pain.

My idea is this. To have desires is natural to humans. So, to crush desires is not natural for humans. But with desires come hopes and expectations. I guess that is all right too. Desires, hopes, expectations, and dreams - they seem to be positive things. If the expectations do not come true, does that necessarily lead to pain or sadness? I say, not necessarily so.

To have desires, expectations and hopes and dreams is something positive to look forward to. But having expectations does not mean that expectations will come true. It is here that there is potential for pain and sadness.

At this stage it is important to realize that there are external factors that we do not determine or control, and yet these factors are crucial for our dreams to come true. So, while it is fine to dream, it is not right to insist that the dreams be fulfilled, because the external forces might not align. Therefore, we must not make our happiness a hostage to the external elements that are crucial for the fulfillment of our dreams.

---

[10] Bowie, MD: Monday, December 12th, 2011.

Doing so will inevitably mean unhappiness because the external elements are not within our control. Unhappiness happens because we find ourselves helpless due to having allowed our happiness to be controlled by the external forces. Because happiness is an internal thing, it is unnatural to subject our happiness to external controls.

Therefore, we should detach our dreams from our happiness. We can dream with the realization that our happiness does not depend upon their fulfillment. Our happiness is in our own hearts, and the achievement of our happiness must remain in our own hands.

When we dream, we construct a blue print for our happiness; therefore, dreams are necessary. However, we are not always good engineers and make mistakes in our blue prints. These mistakes are made via making our dreams rely on the external forces that often work counter to our happiness, and some expressly work towards our unhappiness. Therefore, while we must dream, we must also beware of the external forces, and not allow them to be on the critical path of our happiness. Re-engineer the blue print to keep the entire critical path within your own self, and its control in your own hands. After this, any success is an enhancement to your happiness, and any failure is a lesson in blue print engineering. In both cases, it is a happy journey along the road to self-discovery.

Well-engineered desires that come true make a reality to actualize for us. However, unless we desire, the corresponding reality will not actualize for us. So, dream, little dreamer, dream; have no fear.

*

It occurred to me that life brings us gifts[11]. We should accept them gracefully, with gratitude and thankfulness; and we should enjoy those gifts. However, if life takes a gift away, we should know how to let go; with similar grace. There should be no holding on. We should trust life and let go of this one, and life will bring more gifts to us. Life is a continuing process.

We should accept what good thing happens as a gift; but we should not try to hold on to it. Trying to hold on to it causes us pain, because it is an obstruction to the natural flow of the river of our life. Gifts will come and go because the river must flow.

Two good things that happen in the same contextual sequence are two good things. We should accept both with grace and thankfulness. However, maybe that just one good thing will happen without the other one following it. We should accept the one that life brings us, and not reduce its grace because we lament not getting the second one. A priory, we do not know if it is one gift or a series of gifts. We can desire for one gift to follow another, but trying to insist on it is like holding on to it: like obstructing the flow of the river of life.

We can and should desire all that our heart cares to desire. However, we should let the actual happenings to have an alternative course, and let something happen gracefully that is other than what we anticipated. We should desire but not insist upon its fulfillment. It is a question of the state of our inner self.

---

[11] Antigua, Guatemala: Saturday, December 17, 2011.

This is attachment and detachment at the same time: attachment in the sense of having desires and dreams, and detachment in the sense of not insisting on the results, and letting mother nature take an alternative course. Give the dreams an open space to come alive; and not insist on a particular result. Let life have its way, independent of our wishes, in order to give a natural shape to our dreams. To dream is necessary for life to nurture them. But to insist on one particular outcome of this nurturing is like tying the hands of life, and thereby causing frustration and sadness.

If we insist on our desired results, and hold on to the gifts life has given us while they want to slip away, then we obstruct the flow of life, and limit Nature to give us all she wants to give us. It is like depriving ourselves of gifts that life has for us, by limiting and inhibiting the course of life.

In a sense we should let the child in us to flourish. Children dream, they desire, but the very next moment they move on; and they desire something different, even something opposite. They desire but often do not insist for the desire to come true. If it does, they enjoy it; if it does not, they have another course. Such desiring is detached from the fulfillment of the desire.

Veils, Bubbles, and the Sufi Path

I started some meditation sessions[12]. First one was day before yesterday in the church courtyard of Klein Begijnhof. I sat crossed legs with my hands resting on my knees, and my eyes closed, and my back straight, with my face and eyes pointing straight. I sat there for about an hour. Then I felt to get up. Physically it was a bit hard to get up and start walking, took me like a minute. Walking back, I felt very light, not distracted by people, not focused on anything, just oblivious and contented.

Today I did it twice. In the morning, like 9 am, I sat on the large flat bench along the river branch for a little less than an hour. A thought occurred to me. If there are veils in the outer world, there are perhaps veils also in the inner world, as equivalence principle might suggest. How do we detect these inner veils? That brought the question, how do we detect the outer veils? I thought we detect them after we pass across them to the other side, and realize that they were veils. To detect a veil, therefore, implies crossing the veil to the other side. However, one is pretty content living on this side of the veil, so what is the incentive or motivation for crossing a veil? I am not sure. But I did recall the analogy of a chicken egg hatching; the chicken knocking and breaking the shell.

---

[12] Louvain, Belgium: July 23, 2015.

Why did it break across the shell? Perhaps it is in the nature of the chicken to break the shell? Come to think about it, one can see that for the chicken breaking the shell was a life and death situation. While chicken was momentarily comfortable within the shell, the shell would eventually suffocate the chicken; and by breaking the shell the chicken comes into this great big world. Here, resources never run out for the chicken, though other new risks do appear in this great big world, like being a prey to ravens and cats and humans.

So how do we discover that something is a veil and how do we go across it? What happens if we do not cross this veil? What advantage is derived by going through the veil? What new risks pop up on the other side?

It would seem that there are an infinite number of veils. Everything we can experience or think of or imagine is behind a veil in the sense that, as far as our perception of it is concerned, it is what it is because of the way we interact with it. If our interaction with it changes, then our perception of it changes. It is as if a veil is lifted. Our perception of the things is a veil, that veils their reality from us.

Does there exists something that is not behind a veil? People say God and Truth is not behind a veil, because it is the absolute. However, this is just what people say. God or Truth is not really absolute because human interaction with it is vastly varied, and human perception and conception of it is also vastly varied. What if God and Truth also is behind a veil, or is itself a veil? Then what is behind God-veil or Truth-veil? How do we go across these veils? It feels uncomfortably strange to unveil what is behind God or Truth.

*

Was not sure, but I was bored and did not want to burn time on computer[13]. It was early morning, and decided to go for a walk on the Washington-Baltimore-Annapolis Trail maintained by Baltimore Gas and Electric Company. As soon as I started on the walk, my mind became productively active. I had gone on the same walk in the evening but there was no mental activation. Was it the early morning effect?

I asked myself, why an external company of someone proves pleasing sometimes, the kind of pleasure that is otherwise inaccessible? It occurred to me that we as individuals, each has built a bubble around us based on our self-perception and our world-view which in turn derives from our adopted values. Living in this bubble becomes routine and sometimes boring. An outside person breaks this routine and changes the boredom to happiness. It can even be ecstatic.

What is happening here? You are in your bubble, perhaps bored. Your friend is in his bubble, perhaps bored too. But your friend pulls you out of your bubble into his bubble, so that you find yourself momentarily outside of your bubble, thus feeling freed from the limitations of your own bubble and exalted because of that freedom.

---

[13] Bowie, MD: Thursday, June 28, 2018.

So, you become happy and even ecstatic. You do the same for your friend so that he also feels freed and exalted. This can continue for a time. For how long?

Please realize that you move out of your bubble, into your friend's bubble. Your bubble feels enlarged. You are in another bubble, though it is still only a bubble. It is not an infinite bubble. So, sooner or later another routine sets in, and you find yourself bored, again.

Same happens to your friend.

Each new exciting friend will do this for you. And you will do this for your friend. Each time you meet someone new, you feel freed and exalted for a time, and eventually you set into a routine in your new bubble, albeit a larger one. Again, you feel bored eventually.

There is no sex here, necessarily. We often confuse love with sex and attachment. But love is actually ineffable.

You do not experience this feeling of freedom and exaltation with any arbitrary person; it has to be someone that you can resonate with his bubble, and he can resonate with yours. So, it depends on that person, but more so it depends on your idea of that person. Similarly, it depends upon the other person's idea of you. It happens for both of you when there is an actual or perceived overlap between the two bubbles, your friend's and yours.

And it does not need to be on a one-on-one basis. For example, you can fall in love with a group of idealists, a group of activists, or another group. The principle is the same: an overlap between your bubble and that of the other entity, which is a group in this case, rather than an individual.

This is where travel comes in as a facilitator. Travel brings you in contact with other people, other ideas, other activities, and other groups. You can potentially find overlap with these, and experience freedom and exaltation because of it. There is often nothing forcing you together; you come together voluntarily, so that the affinity is mutual.

The process repeats itself. Each time, a routine can set in eventually, and you can feel bored, again. To address this situation, you can do something like the following. Keep meeting new friends, ideas, activities, and groups. If you travel, this should become relatively easier. If you travel long enough and wide enough, you will never run out of possibilities. This is obviously a possible route to take. But it leaves a track of excitements turned into boredom, perhaps not a pretty sight to look back to.

Remember why the situation arises. It is because your own bubble is small and restrictive. And likewise, your friend's bubble also is small and restrictive. So, one might work on this smallness and restrictiveness.

Get to know yourself by exploring your own inner self, by way of self-discovery. Your inner self is potentially very large, and unrestrictive. You discover yourself through becoming aware of your own 'self' via looking inward. Because there is an infinite space to discover, this can continue indefinitely: ever discovering a new you, and never running out of these discoveries. Rather, the discoveries become progressively more exciting and more meaningful. There never is a time to get bored!

More you become aware of what is actually out there within your 'self', the more 'friends' you have to enlarge your bubble. And as you move forward, saying hello to your new friends, and leaving behind the old ones, you can occasionally look back and there is nothing to regret because you realize it is the same friend with whom you have been throughout! Only that friend is the real you, that has evolved with you to expand your freedom and the scope of your exaltation.

When we recall the equivalence principle, we also realize that when our inner-self is our friend, the world beyond is also our friend. When we love and possess the inner world, we also love and possess the outer world.

*

Woke up around 6:30 am[14]. After tea, went for a walk on WB&A trail towards Rt 193.

First, I thought about Sufism; how the first Station is Sayre and Suluk. The station starts after the Taube, meaning a realization that you have been too engrossed in the outward world and you need to return to explore the inner world. It seems Sufism starts the process by reorienting us from the outward world towards the inward world.

The first station after Taube is Sayre and Suluk. Sayre means to go around observing, seeing, and witnessing things, events, and phenomena. As you witness these things, some of the things attract your attention and you go to observe them more closely. For example, your

---

[14] Bowie, MD: Monday, July 09, 2018.

attention goes to an unusually beautiful tree, a fire place chimney, dead worms on the trail, and grass growing on asphalted surfaces. As you observe these selected things and go from one of them to the next, your Sayre becomes Suluk which means a journey.

Thus, every life is a journey.

What happens during Sayre and Suluk? We all live in our bubbles. As you go places and observe the happenings, some observations challenge your bubble. When the bubble is challenged often enough and severely enough, the bubble eventually bursts. When the bubble bursts, in Sufi parlance it is said that a veil is removed. Now, you see more clearly, more transparently, you see farther, and you see more things. Now you are in a bigger bubble. It is like a baby chicken has broken through the egg shell and is born into a great big world.

It seems you are always in a bubble.

When you have popped enough bubbles, in Sufism it is said that you have entered Berzekh. Berzekh means a wall that separates two states of being: you are not awake yet but you are not asleep either. The signs are that you have popped the bubble of your ego. After popping the bubble of ego, you enter the station of Berzekh, where you continue to further work on the ego. Sufism says that ego hides in unimaginable places. In your spiritual journey through Berzekh, you discover all such places, and you empty your "self" of the ego. When are you done emptying the ego? It is when your Pir-o-Murshid determines that you are done.

Eventually, everything is a judgment call.

The next stage is to kill your "will". You have no will; the freedom to act is an illusion. You have no freedom; everything is the will of God.

If something bad happens, it is not the will of God; you caused it to happen because you exercised your will because of your ego that is still around. So, if you are hit by a misfortune, it is your doing; but if you decide to do something about it, then you are violating the concept that in reality you have no freedom to act. So, the test of your state and your inner values is in the forefront at this station.

There are contradictions along the way.

In Sufism there is no "understanding"; there is only "experiencing" by being there and "witnessing" it.

What I call inner values and contradictions, they are perhaps Zen Koans. The purpose is to help the individual escape himself from thinking, and escape the constraints of the rational mind. You kill your rational self and you fully submit yourself to the experience of God, as shown to you by the Pir-o-Murshid through the things you witness. You have annihilated your existence in the existence of God. Sufis call it Fina-Fi-Allah.

In my mind the role of a pir-o-murshid is possibly troublesome. If a pir is involved you are really submitting yourself to the pir, not necessarily to God. This opens the door for a fake pir to exploit. If no pir is involved you are submitting yourself to 'something' of your own making. If you are not sufficiently mature, then your own making can mislead you, or even kill you. If the pir is not sincere, it too can mislead you, or even kill you.

It is dangerous territory!

When you are in Fina-Fi-Allah, are you still in a bubble? Not sure what Sufis say about veils at this stage. But I think all these Muqamat and Ahwal that Sufis talk about are man-made concepts. They are veils in themselves; they are bubbles in which a person with Fina-Fi-Allah lives.

When you are dead as a mortal being, after having killed your ego and having killed your reliance on the rational ways, you have submitted yourself totally to God. What does God do in turn? I am not sure. There is too much noise here. But Sufis believe that God revives you from your death, so that you have a life with God. It is like Christ having died and resurrected and then raised to God and now sitting on the right hand of God. Sufis refer this as Baqa-Bi-Allah, existing with God.

A person then returns back to the world of greed and impurity, but he is untouched by it because he is also existing with God. Again, there is much noise. It is like the second coming of Christ. Sufis call it Baqa-Bin-Naas, existing with people. Mohammad was the best example of Baqa-Bin-Naas: he was totally with God via being totally with people. God and people converge through this state, sort of in some Equivalence relationship[15].

---

15 Note added during editing, May 12, 2023: I have stated clearly and categorically that the spiritual way, as presented in this book, is for the entire humanity irrespective if one is religious or not, atheist or theist, and agnostic or gnostic. I have talked about God while talking about Sufis because it is unavoidable.

Roaming (Sayre)

What is it that I search[16]? Don't know if I am searching for something, but I am searching! Is it a thing, is it a person, is it a state of being, is it an answer? What? What keeps me roaming? It is clear that my search keeps me roaming. But the search itself is not understood. If I stand still, I expect nothing new to happen. By roaming, I expect some new things to happen. I need new happenings, for the old happenings have not even provided me with questions, not to talk about answers. It is perhaps like this: go roam around the world, and see the signs. If I see some signs, I expect them to trigger thoughts, and maybe it will lead to some answers. Answers like, what am I searching for?

What do I want? I don't want anything that I can think of. Sex, romance, thrill, adventure, nirvana? The answer is no. It is perhaps something I have not even thought of! The search and roaming both are undefined, completely open ended. Perhaps the roaming will tell what I am searching for. The search, the journey, will start after that.

Who I want to be? I want to be myself. But what is my 'self'? They say knowing 'self' is knowing 'god'. Is it that the two are practically the same thing, two words for the same thing? In some obscure way, in some

---

[16] San Pedro La Laguna, Guatemala: November 16, 2011.

limited sense, I tend to think, for now, that there is some vital connection. Some questions of detail remain.

Roaming around in the physical space is perhaps incomplete. I have to roam into people's mind, those who have roamed farther than me, those who have some glimpse of what they search for, and what they don't search for.

It is important to stand 'naked' in the sense of having nothing to hide, and being happy with who we are. When I listen to the poem by Faiz, "aaj bazaar mein pa be jaulan chalo[17]", that poem brings this nakedness to mind. It is important to have done that walking; to stand naked before the society, the people, the friends, and the family. I am reaching in a frame that can be more receptive, more communicative, on such matters.

I look for people who have roamed farther than me, but I have not met many. I have met a few who have roamed far and wide. Mostly I meet the young tourists, sometimes with self-discovery in mind. I have also met some older folks, still walking in non-spiritual ways. I try to learn from everybody, in terms of things they offer and things they do not offer.

---

[17] Note added during editing, May 26, 2023: It is a line from an Urdu poem by Faiz Ahmad Faiz. This line seems to say: Now the time has come that you walk in the market place, in front of everyone, with chains around your feet.

Journeying (Suluk)

Has been three months here in Oaxaca[18]. I think it was a good three months: had the experiential manifestations in San Jose del Pacifico, came across so many new and wonderful things, met wonderful people, and unexpected experiences. Everything helped me grow a little bit, everything had a spiritual side. I should sort of digest it at the end. Though analytic approach is probably not helpful in this context; will see.

I sometimes think about what Adi says: submit your will, have no desires and plans, silence the mind, stay still, and remain silent. But many spiritual people like Pope are intent on practical matters. Most spiritual people do seem to have gone into practical things like preaching. They seem to have done it after having first acquired spiritual enlightenment.

Inside, I am torn between these two things: acquiring spirituality and launching practical projects. Do we really acquire spirituality and then go into practical matters like launching reformation and emancipation projects? In that case, when is it that we finish acquiring spirituality? My answer is that we never finish acquiring spiritual

---

[18] Oaxaca, Mexico: Tuesday, December 12, 2017.

enlightenment! At what stage then do we get into launching practical projects like preaching, teaching, reformation, and emancipation?

Maybe it is the Equivalence Principle throwing a monkey wrench here! Maybe it is Nature's way to teach me something new? Maybe the puzzle is an answer to my seeking? Do we know and recognize an answer when we see it? Do we know a lesson, a pointer, an answer when they come to us? How are we supposed to deal with, and what are we supposed to do with such lessons, pointers, and answers?

We are always supposed to listen to our inner self. We are supposed to continue being ourself! We are not supposed to have an anxiety. We must not have a fear that we might miss an answer, misunderstand a pointer, and miss learning a lesson. First, we are supposed to not let fear become our driver. So, let me keep flowing forward in time without anxiety or fear.

Is this act of flowing just like the flow of a river that submits itself fully to gravity; to let gravity take it wherever? Or is the human flow different, with a conscious urge to steer, seek and reach?

This also leads to another puzzle! Maybe it is the same puzzle manifesting again, namely the priority between inward journey and external project-oriented activities?

We need a "complete" set of "bases elements" in order to describe life fully and completely. Some bases elements are easy and obvious to glean from the external world, like the obvious need for survival, and these same elements would be relatively difficult to discover by looking inwards. There are elements in the inward view, like our passions and desire for happiness and fulfillment, and these elements would be relatively difficult to glean from an external looking view. We must do both, inward journey and external projects, simultaneously in order to obtain a complete set of bases elements. As regards the issue of priority, both actions, namely looking inward and looking outward, must go on in parallel, simultaneously[19].

Therefore, I must do both in order to discover a complete set of bases elements to be able to formulate everything in life, to discover the spiritual way to living, which is both inward and outward! So, we must simultaneously look inwards and look outwards: both have essential and vital functions in our lives, and each provides the essential elements that together constitute a complete set for a "spiritual way" to living. Without either one, the set might remain incomplete, and the spiritual way to living might remain wanting.

It also hints at solving the other puzzle: that between actively using the mind versus silencing the mind; between launching projects and staying still. At a certain stage of enlightenment and human development, actively using the mind is looking outwards, and silencing the mind is looking inwards. We must do both! But how? At any given moment, the mind is either active or silent! So, there must be an actual transition taking place for the mind to be active or silent. While on the spiritual journey, the active mind uses the analytic process, and the still mind uses the "witnessing" of experiential demonstrations.

---

[19] Note added while editing, May 29, 2023: When there is a race condition that arises between an inner spiritual pursuit and an external project, this can be resolved by the contextual circumstances. Such a situation is never on the critical path of a journey.

In my case, silencing the mind was achieved first by Marijuana in San Pedro La Laguna in Guatemala, and then by Mushrooms in San Jose del Pacifico in Mexico! Details will be described under "Witnessing Experiments" beginning on page 95.

Would my mind make a transition to silence without the intervention of the psychedelics? In my case, it has not happened without the psychedelics except possibly once when I had a very brief encounter with "silence" and "stillness" as is described towards the end in the essay on "Seekers of the Spiritual" on page 29. I think my training as a theoretical physicist is a particular source for the need of psychedelics to silence the mind.

As is described under "Witnessing Experiments", at times a silent mind state is more perceptive than the active mind state! It would seem that such a silent mind state is a form of meta-physical state: a spiritual state that is more amenable to receive and witness an experiential demonstration. If so, can the silent mind state be sufficient? Must we also have the active mind state?

The active mind state invokes an urge to 'seek'. This urge to seek determines the content of the experiential demonstration that we witness during the silent mind state. We will not get our answers without consciously, via the active mind state, seeking and asking! That is why people's psychedelic experiences differ widely, based on what they seek.

This urge to seek can also be planted in someone by a guru, teacher, or pir-o-murshid. If this route is taken, the danger is that the external suggestion by a corrupt teacher can manipulate the active mind state, and consequently also the silent mind state. Therefore, a safer route is for us to self-motivate ourself in our urges and seeking, by looking inwards into our inner self. Everybody can do it through contemplation using the active mind state, which is the default state of the mind.

It is also true that it is necessary for the mind to make a transition to a silent mind state in order to witness the experiential demonstration to make spiritual progress! The active mind state, the default state, will not fully produce this spiritual content.

We must get some essential elements from the physical world and some from the spiritual world: just one world does not suffice in practice. The value of the Equivalence Principle, therefore, is to reveal to us the physical meanings of the spiritual world and the spiritual meanings of the physical world. The revelation of such unified meanings is after the fact; it is guided and helped by the explicit invocation of the Equivalence Principle. The presence and significance of the equivalence principle becomes a common knowledge for all travelers after they reach a level of contemplative stage in their journey.

Thoughts

I took to a walk in the morning around 9 am[20]. It had been on my mind to find out how to look along the inward dimension. Anytime I tried to think or meditate, I found myself thinking thoughts that resembled the outer dimension, the physical world. So how do I turn inwards to discover my spirituality, and to enhance it?

This is important because it is at the heart of my theory of spirituality. So, as I practiced this theory by looking inward, I repeatedly found myself looking at the physical world instead.

I started to contemplate on what is meditation, what is thinking, what is thought? Why do we think? What does it mean to think?

During the walk I thought to myself: what does it mean to think? I came to the idea that one thinks because one is alive. It is a result of being alive. It happens like other things happen in the process of living. It happens like breathing happens, like eating happens, like walking happens.

So, is there a meaning to the process of thinking? Is there a meaning to breathing, eating, walking? These things happen without one consciously realizing their purpose, their meaning. Nevertheless,

---

[20] Bowie, MD: July 31, 2014. (Discourse: Thinking and Skills (073114))

they have a meaning, they have a purpose. So, what is the meaning of thinking? What is the purpose of thinking?

I came up with a short answer. Thinking means that questions come to mind, and answers come to mind; not necessarily together and not necessarily in that order; not necessarily correlated, not necessarily in any order. If we look at children, maybe they do not think of any questions or answers. Maybe they think of dreamy possibilities, possibilities that they wish for. Implicitly, they are also thinking to answer their desires and dreams; though not explicitly in the format of questions or answers. The vocabulary of the children is different from that of the grownups. However, the biological processes behind the thoughts are perhaps similar in children and in adults. Our skills and training and experiences in life give our thinking the format of questions and answers.

Does thinking have a purpose? It must have a purpose if the processes of life have a purpose. What is the purpose of breathing? I guess it is to maintain life. What is the purpose of eating? It too is to maintain life, though apparently it is in response to hunger. What is the purpose of walking? I guess that too is to maintain life, though apparently it is to reach somewhere to satisfy some need associated with the maintenance of life. Similarly, the purpose of thinking also is to maintain life, though apparently it is to satisfy a question posed by life.

Life induces thinking and it also consummates the product of thinking. From a spiritual perspective, examples of thoughts can be such questions: What does happiness mean to me? What does fulfillment mean to me? What does peace mean to me? What do I desire? What are my passions? How do I become happy? How do I feel peacefulness? What will make me feel fulfilled? What will satisfy my desires? What will fulfill my passions?

Feelings

After some deliberation, it seems that a feeling is a response by life to a stimulus generated by the process of living[21].

It seems that, at a raw level, this response that we call feeling happens immediately after the occurrence of the stimulus; it is almost instantaneous. Hence there seems to be no thinking or deliberation involved in generating the feeling.

Now the response (feeling) depends on the nature of the stimulus. Hence some selection process must occur to evaluate the stimulus and to generate the appropriate feeling that corresponds to the stimulus. This selection process seems to be non-intellectual in nature because the intellectual processes take longer deliberation to arrive at a decision for action. Hence this selection process is largely biological, at a raw level.

Examples of feelings are the feelings of pleasure and the feelings of pain. For example, we may feel pain when we are sick or when we are injured. We may feel pleasure when we eat a delicious meal or we are in a romantic company.

The stimuli that generate feelings may be from within ourselves or they may be externally generated. Examples of internal stimuli are the conditions of sickness and health. Examples of external stimuli are the

---

[21] Bowie, MD: August 1st, 2014. (Discourse: Feeling (080114))

attitude of other people with respect to us, and our own attitude towards other people.

Our thoughts can also serve as the stimuli, and that can result in the generation of corresponding feelings. For instance, we may feel pleasure in thinking about a delicious romantic dinner, and we may feel pain in thinking about death and injury.

On the other hand, feeling can generate thoughts. If we feel pleasure, it may induce us to think about pleasure and the scenarios associated with it. If we feel pain, it may induce us to think about this pain and its causes. Thus, feelings are generated by stimuli, and they themselves can act like stimuli to generate thoughts. In such situations thoughts are like feelings.

Conscience and Intellect

Some actions are involuntary, like the action of the heart or the knee-jerk reaction under which the foot moves when the doctor gently hits the knee[22].

However, most human actions during the process of living are voluntary in nature. They are the results of intellectual thinking and deliberations. Examples of such processes include pursuits for a livelihood, pursuits for pleasure, and pursuits for spirituality. The innate capabilities of man are there to fully assist in these actions.

The voluntary actions take the following course. First our senses observe our environment. These observations enter our intellect for processing. This processing is a function of our world-view. Our world-view is formed as a result of the values of our society, our training, our personal experiences, and our own values. All these factors, and many sub-factors, influence the manner in which we process the observations from our senses. Finally, we decide the nature and scope of our voluntary action. Often multiple courses of action exist as possibilities. Our world-view leads our intellect to pick a particular course of action based on our perception of its optimality.

---

[22] Bowie, MD: August 1st, 2014. (Discourse: Action (080114))

In simplistic terms, our idea of optimality derives from a cost-benefit type analysis based on what we perceive as benefit and what we perceive as cost. These concepts are often handed down to us by the society we grow up in, and the religion into which we are born.

These concepts often include what is stated as the golden rule: do unto others as you would have them do unto you. This is the ethics of reciprocity. This is as far as the intellect would go. The intellect and the world-view of most people do not even go that far; the happenings in the world now adays bear plenty of witness on this, as they fall short of the golden rule.

To go beyond this, we need to go beyond the physical realm and make a call on our spiritual realm. One thing in our spiritual realm that will immediately hold our hand is our conscience. Please note that our conscience is different from our consciousness.

Our conscience is purely spiritual in nature. For it to hold our hand, all we have to do is to let it hold our hand. We make a conscious decision to live according to the song of our own conscience, the voice of our heart. For that purpose, we need no guru, we need no teacher, and we need no special training. All we need is our own self and our own commitment to live our conscience. Our conscience was born with us. It is uniquely ours; it is not the same as the conscience of another person. We were born that way; our conscience was born uniquely for us when we were born.

*

The ethics of reciprocity, as discussed above, is a primitive ethics; it is the product of a utilitarian world-view[23]. It is fraught with problems. For example, if our intellect computes that we can behave unethically and yet we can escape the consequences of the law through some clever maneuvering, then our intellect can lead us to drop the utilitarian ethics. Only the future will tell if we actually managed to escape the consequences of being unethical. If we fail to escape, we suffer the consequences. The golden rule is therefore not enough as a basis for ethics. It merely diverts attention from the real ethics and it also diverts attention from the flaws in the utilitarian ethics represented by the golden rule.

The intellect is therefore not complete, rather it is faulty, as a basis for an ethical life. There is a need to go beyond the intellect in order to achieve a foundation for our ethical living, and the achievement of our peace, happiness and fulfillment. We need to go beyond the physical realm and make a call on our spiritual realm. One thing in our spiritual realm that will immediately hold our hand is our conscience.

The intellect is like a giant computing machinery. It can compute and evaluate, but it does not contain within itself the criteria for computation and evaluation. That function is provided by the conscience.

Conscience is the human capability to tell a "right" thing apart from a "wrong" thing. The capability lives latent within a person, and we give it the name "conscience". Conscience is not a catalogue of things

---

[23] Bowie, MD: August 10th, 2014. (Post 19: Intellect versus Conscience August 10, 2014.)

labeled as right or wrong; rather it is the capability to label a thing as right or wrong within a context.

Our conscience will warn us when we do a wrong thing, and it will appreciate us when we do a right thing. The right things enhance the happiness and fulfillment in our life; the wrong things diminish our happiness and fulfillment by bringing us unhappiness and frustration. The state of happiness and fulfillment during our lifespan will therefore serve as a litmus test for us to know our right and wrong behavior.

Our conscience may label apparently the same thing as right in one situation and wrong in another. Our conscience knows and it is a spiritual art to be able to listen to it. As the intellect envelops the senses and enables them to function correctly, similarly the conscience envelops the intellect and enables it to function correctly. When our intellect functions correctly, it makes decisions that enhance our happiness, peace, and fulfillment.

We need both the conscience and the intellect because the intellect does not understand our happiness, it does not understand what makes us at peace, and it does not know how to make us feel fulfilled. The conscience knows these things, and it can guide the intellect to bring our life into balance. In other words, the intellect cannot work without a comprehensive infrastructure within man that supports the intellectual decision-making towards a balanced life: a life of peace, fulfillment, and happiness. This comprehensive infrastructure is referred to as the conscience.

We need two things: our conscience and our intellect. Everybody has them, beginning from birth. We do not need a guru or a spiritual leader. We are our guru; we are our spiritual leader. We can trust ourself, use our intellect, and listen to our conscience[24].

---

[24] Note added while editing, 29th May 2023. While we need no guru, we surely need the learning processes because learning continues from cradle to casket. We learn from people, from books, from life situations, from observing the signs around us, and from listening to our conscience. We learn and make our own decisions, and we also are responsible for them. Nobody else is responsible for our personal decisions, and nobody else should be making them for us.

Adding up Life

I am a traveler[25]. To where am I travelling? That I don't know! Do I want to know? That also I don't know? Do I want to ask why? Do I want to ask why not? Or do I want to just travel and ask nothing?

In this discourse travel is not just the travelling that I am doing; it is a metaphor for living the life, the journey of life, the journey that is life.

I see creation, the marvels of it, the wonders of it, the simple complexity of it, the orderly disorder of it, the disorderly order of it, the beauty of it, the ugliness of it, all of it! And I cannot understand that there is no Creator of all this. The Creator has veiled itself well, behind the orderly laws of science that seem to run it without a Creator. But the laws themselves are part of the Creation, and these laws do not run by themselves, without a design behind them that makes them work together interoperably, in a self-healing flawless manner. As a Physicist, I cannot see how there is no Creator behind this veil of Creation. That is my take; your take may be different.

All right, let us grant that there is a Creator. So what? What does it mean that there is a Creator? Should I care? Does this Creator care that I should care? That there is a Creator is just a fact. It does not have

---

[25] Bowie, MD: November 1st, 2011.

to extrapolate beyond that. The usual course of enquiring regarding why the Creator created us, and what is our obligation to this Creator, is actually an artifact of man's manipulations of man. It is a manifestation of a blasphemy, whereby man claims to know the mind of this Creator, before he even knows the rudiments of who this Creator is. Usually, this claim is made in such a tacit way so that it would not look like a blasphemy; namely, by claiming that the Creator himself has told this to man through his prophets and scriptures; or even by claiming that this Creator came disguised as a man and told us so. Such tactics work because of the mastery of the Clergy at manipulation, even if with good intentions. In addition, there has been a collusion between the Clergy and the Kings to coordinate the exploitation of the people for mutual benefits.

Is finding about this Creator the same thing as finding about one's spirituality? What I care about, and should care about, is the "innerness" within me that my heart feels and yearns. That is the inner thoughts, inner questions, inner peace, inner turbulence. There is all of this within me. That is my 'inner-self'. Is dealing with this 'inner-self' the same thing as dealing with this Creator?

There are questions within me, desires within me, longing within me, and a sort of unfulfilled searching within me. I call that the 'spirituality' within me. The pursuit of my inner-self is the journey of life; I also call it the "spirituality" within me. The three things – my inner-self, the journey of my life on the spiritual-way, and my spirituality – are the same thing. In a way of parlance, the three things are synonymous for the purpose of my discourses.

For now, the intention is to fulfill the inner-self by journeying on the spiritual way. I hesitate to call it a goal, for goals are in reference to the external world, and we are addressing the inner-self. This fulfillment of the inner-self is an internal pursuit. The Creator that we talked about may be relevant in this pursuit only if this Creator is, at least partially, part of my inner-self.

Other than that, the journey for the inner-self is very open ended and rather somewhat amorphous in nature. Perhaps this journey is open ended because life itself is open ended, till death ends it. Similarly, the journey is amorphous because we begin life with a clean slate, and it crystallizes out only as we live it. More we live life, more it crystallizes, and takes beautiful shapes. Does it ever finish the crystallization? Is the pursuit ever fully accomplished? I do not know if that stage is possible. Did Buddha completely accomplish this, did Christ completely accomplish this? For living an individual life, what is important is to live a peaceful, happy, and fulfilling life while pursuing the accomplishment on the spiritual way. We will discover at the end how much we did accomplish. Life is not comparative; each life is lived in its own positive pursuit.

What is this journey then? It is likely that it is neither completely accomplishable nor its result crystallizable because the results are mostly ineffable? My take is this: irrespective of its conclusion or crystallization, the journey has to be pursued because we are alive and the inside of us insists that it be pursued. It has to be travelled for its own sake.

One might argue that I have been living all along without pursuing this journey in a deliberate way. Nevertheless, during this life I have accomplished few things like wife, children, education, wealth, and community relations. However, these things are external. If I have not heeded the innerness of me, then inside I have not lived all this time. That is like I have been rowing someone else's boat for their pleasure, and my role was simply to row it for their pleasure – I have not discovered and explored my own pleasure, my own happiness, my own fulfillment, and my own peacefulness. This may not be entirely true. Some of my inner self is accomplished through the external world like family and friends and activities that I cherish. To a proportional extent, I have accomplished my happiness, fulfillment, and peace.

There is much that remains to be pursued along my spiritual way. There is no hurry and there is no eagerness. There is no fear of not accomplishing it. Every journey is travelled in its own right. Important thing is to travel the "way", not necessarily to reach somewhere like a destination; places and epochs along the way are only incidental, the real accomplishment is within.

Things are so intertwined that it is hard to separate them, and I do not know how to add them up for the "living" that I have done in my life. As I illustrated above, I accomplished some living even while rowing someone else's boat for their pleasure. I might have been doing things that did not resonate with my inner self, but I might have done them out of love for those that I genuinely did love. However, such fine-tuned accounting is unnecessary, because my conscience knows how much living I have done, and my heart knows how much I have pursued my innerness. What we feel within our inner self, deep within our hearts, that is what counts. It is the conscience that speaks the last words.

Therefore, I am conducting experiments on my life, while journeying on my spiritual way, in order to make my life into genuine living. These experiments will change some things within me; in my conscience, they will change the way I feel with respect to my own life. This conscientious feeling will be the success criterion for my experiments: if they help me answer my inner questions, if they produce inner peace, fulfilment, and happiness. My heart knows my inner feelings of being alive.

Witnessing Experiments

At the Barber Shop

Arrived in San Pedro La Laguna last night[26]. Went around and reached the waterfront. Met two young guys. One Juan named after the Pope when he visited Guatemala in 1983. The other an American from Baltimore area, a Jewish kid named Daniel around 38 years of age, who has lived in San Pedro for 5 or 6 years. Daniel makes jewelry from threads and stones. Juan is also an artist but has a barber shop. Daniel and Juan are friends. Daniel displays his jewelry outside the barber shop, located on the main tourist street near the water.

I went with them to the shop, to see the jewelry. In the morning I had seen a young kid, perhaps named Obule, who had talked to me on the way to bank, earlier this morning. He came to the barber shop and had his hair cut like a long pony in the middle and shaved off on either side. The kid who took me to the Hotel Peneleu last night, also passed by there and said hello; I met him like three times today. Then like 4 or 5 kids came to see him from Guatemala City (simply known as The City).

Earlier on the waterfront, as soon as he saw me approaching, Juan had asked me if I want high or low, to which I had answered that I like where I am at. Then Juan, Daniel, and myself walked to his barber shop,

---

[26] San Pedro de Laguna, Guatemala: December 4, 2011.

about a block away. He said he cuts hair very good, but only when he is high. I told him that I have not eaten anything and have to eat breakfast. He took me to the neighboring place where we got egg omelet, bread, and beans. Brought it to the shop and ate there. I left some bread and beans and Daniel ate that. He said that he ate breakfast but he had had to work 5 hours and can eat more.

Daniel is making a cover and carrier for a cigarette lighter for Juan, using the threads that Daniel uses for his jewelry. He braids threads together to hold the precious stones for bracelets and necklaces; he uses no glue. He collects his stones during his travels.

Juan started making a cigarette from the weed that grows in Guatemala. A guy came in and he asked him if he wanted high. They went in the backyard. He came back and said to me 'go and get high'. There were a guy, two girls, and three of us. The cigarette passed around between the six of us. Perhaps three cigarettes went around. I may have taken like 8 puffs. I had previously tried some weed, when Ramin lit a pipe and I had taken 3 or 4 puffs from his pipe. That had made me laugh continuously, and then after less than an hour I had passed out. I was stoned, then I woke up and went to the toilet; and he later took me to a coffee place where they have coffee that 'wakes' you up.

But this time it was totally different. Perhaps it was a different weed. After less than an hour I felt I was dosing off. I feared I will pass out. I went to the rug near the small speakers to which Juan's iPod was connected. I gradually laid down there. I did not pass out, I was awake.

But reality started to change, first the yellow orange and red colors became unusually bright. Then I started to feel that the life around me was like a performance on the stage. Nothing was clear. Everything I thought was happening, something different, and sometimes some totally opposite thing also seemed to be happening. First, I thought the room of the barber shop was the world theater and people passing from the street or people who came in from the street were actors. Then I thought the people in the shop were also actors. I thought about myself as an observer; an observer who was part of the act.

People came in, some got weeds. I thought the barber shop was a front for selling weed. But few people came and Juan cut their hair with as much dedication. Daniel kept at his jewelry making thread work. Juan and Daniel kept doing their things, as if they just wanted to do these things but did not care if people came for the barber shop or not, if people got weeds or not. As if they were indifferent to the money part of the whole thing. They lighted weed cigarettes and offered to the in comers, apparently free. They also lighted something, blew it off, and put a glass on the smoke. Then they inhaled the marijuana smoke.

I lay there for hours. I had come there like 9.30 am and it was late evening. Things were happening. And I understood everything. But this understanding was very clear, like an intense insight, how contradictions were not contradictions, how things were happening randomly and then fitting into a great big picture, as if the result was planned or engineered. Flashes of understanding would suddenly appear to me and then it would be gone as quickly. If I stressed to think what I understood a moment before, sometimes I could recall but only partially. It was sequence of things happening, each thing producing a different flash of insight, and then the flash is gone, and another flash happens. During a flash-understanding, things were perfect, beautiful, and open in their purpose. Things were happening randomly, yet under a scheme, and nothing was right, nothing was wrong, everything was like it was meant to be. Just that, one thing was because of another thing happening, and that was the way things happened; no right, no wrong, just perfection, just beauty.

It appeared things were happening because somebody desired them to happen; and if somebody desired something, the thing happened.

I saw how quantum mechanical view happened: of things composing of each other; of collapsing of probability because someone desired something.

I saw how people were going to 'god' as a volunteer, but inevitable was happening. I wondered, this god people were gravitating to, if this god was there because people were gravitating to it, or people were gravitating to it because this god was there. I suddenly understood, rather experienced, the Quranic assertion: you will be brought back to me. It was demonstrated to me.

At many occasions I understood a 'proof' that god exists. But the experience and understanding would quickly disappear.

After like 3 pm I woke up. But the sequence of happenings continued. Very often it would appear that I am waking up, reality is returning, and I would fear that this spiritual happening of insightfulness was ending. But it would come back. The things that were happening in the shop would revert back to 'flashes' of understanding, flashes of a perfect world in which nothing needed to be changed. I would try to understand and glean some wisdom, but it would always come back to this: there was no understanding of these things, there was no nugget of wisdom to be gathered.

It appeared that an attempt to understand things tended to spoil the perfection of the world. Things were true without any notion of judgement. Things happened because world was perfect, and because world was perfect so things happened the way they did. Everybody was right, no matter what he or she was doing, no matter what anybody was doing, everybody was right. I understood: how it takes all sorts to make the world.

It appeared to me that Juan, Daniel, and all other people were there to give me these flashes of the reality. Many times, Juan and Daniel turned to me and spoke to me, and their actions and words fitted into the happening that I was experiencing at the moment. It was as if they knew what I was experiencing, and they were helping me to understand what was happening.

Juan pretended to play music and sing, and then said it is all hands-free, music is not playing, but it is coming out because I desired it to happen and the desire makes it happen. Daniel laughed and turned to me saying things like 'it is intense', and it was indeed intense for me what was happening at the moment. It was as if they knew what I was going through. But they were doing what they were doing without knowing my condition, and it was all put together into a perfect picture by an unseen hand.

When I got up, Daniel lit up some marijuana and I took the smoke. That did not seem to do much to me.

I came out around 5:30 pm. Walked a little. Had dinner. And came to the hotel.

This was the first ever happening with me. I felt I was like Arjun in Mahabharata and Krishna was showing me the reality of the things.

Everything that I thought was a paradox, or contradiction, resolved itself in the flashes that I experienced in the Barber Shop.

I thought analytic understanding was in its own trapping, and experiencing 'it' was the only way to know. I experienced the world in the Barber Shop: I did not understand the world; the experiencing seemed to obviate understanding. Understanding seemed disjointed from experiencing. You could experience without understanding. The experiencing resolved the difficulties of understanding, without producing an understanding; rather, making understanding irrelevant. I thought that the desire to understanding was merely a reflection of lack of experiencing.

*

The above[27] is the exact description as I had written it down then. I changed some punctuations, but did not change the wording except to correct spelling. This was my first spiritual "witnessing-experience"

---

[27] I added this note on January 9th, 2023.

episode. It was a moment of enlightenment. I have never been the same after that. Since this experience, I have felt free and without fear. The experience, rather witnessing, is within me in a way that I do not understand. I can recall that this "witnessing experience" had opened my eyes and removed gaps and difficulties that I had in my understanding of the world and the life. However, this understanding did not stay with me; I am no wiser as a result of this, at least not in a way that I recognize. However, I am free and fearless as a result of this episode, and I am left with the realization that understanding is like training wheels on a bicycle, and real riding is through "witnessing experience".

A Vision

I was having late lunch or early dinner with Tomoko Seiyo when Juan and Daniel showed up[28]. Juan had a drink with us and Daniel went to wind down his jewelry display and then returned.

We went to the lakeside and lit a cigarette. I had few puffs, and it started to affect me after less than half an hour. I said I will make a move, and we all returned. Me and Tomoko hired a tuk tuk to the hostel.

She did not come with me to my room, though I asked her to come for half an hour. I came and went to bed. In a condition between sleep and wakefulness I had a sort of a vision of wisdom. I woke up around 9:45 and I was fully awake, still remembering the wisdom revealed to me during this vision. I started to write it down.

It started with me thinking about Tomoko. Will she come to me, what if she comes to me, should I expect and desire that she comes to me? If I desire, does it not imply the possibility of pain of unfulfilled desire? But to desire seems natural to man. Is man destined to suffer the pain of unfulfilled desires?

What if she comes, do I fear what if she comes? What if I desire her to come?

---

[28] San Pedro de Laguna, Guatemala: Tuesday, December 6, 2011.

I received the answer that we should both be free to act our conscience. To make the two actions meet in the middle and lead to the desired result, that is the role of God. We will act our conscience but leave the results to God; God alone will make it happen. If we take it upon ourselves to make it happen, it can lead to pain of failure of our struggle. We must struggle to make it happen, but we also must leave the outcome to God.

All right, we must not take it upon ourselves to make it happen, and thus not suffer pain of failure. But what does it mean to act our conscience? That seems to mean that we make the decisions of our lives according to the 'inner voice of conscience'. We act according to our conscience, we struggle according to our conscience, and then we leave the outcome to God. It is the role of God to take the struggle to completion or not.

Our conscience too is not clearly known to us. We may decide according to the false notions of our religion, upbringing, education, and societal conditioning. And we may confuse it with acting our conscience, because we do not know any better. All right, here is our responsibility to 'know' our conscience. I recall a saying that to know our "self" (conscience) is to know our God. Neither one is easy. But to know is our responsibility. We must frequently undertake the "inward" journey to know our "self" (conscience).

How do we know our conscience? That is equivalent to knowing if our decision is according to our true inner voice or it is according to our conditioning. To the extent that our conditioning has led us away from our conscience, our life's decisions would be 'wrong'. How do we know if our life's decisions are right or wrong, in order to know our conscience? Our decision being right or wrong is not according to some warm and fuzzy feelings we may feel. The answer is to be derived from four criteria: scientific criteria; inter-human moral criteria; spiritual meditation criteria; and over all internal consistency criteria of the entire framework of one's thought process. More on these criteria later.

So, the answer is that we know our conscience gradually by evaluating our life's decisions and correcting them when necessary. When all our life's decisions are correct then we have understood our conscience; and we have understood our God. At this stage our conscience represents God, and the decisions of our conscience are decisions of God. They must therefore conclude in success. That is the meaning of the statement that when man reaches closeness with God then God becomes the hands and feet and eyes and hearing of that man. The conscience of that man effectively becomes the will of God. Yes, God is within us. The only God we acknowledge is the God we have within us.

A general state of conscience is that of incomplete understanding of our conscience. To the extent that we understand our conscience, indeed we understand our God to that extent. God is a very personal God. To the extent that we do not understand our conscience, to that extent we do not know the God within us. To the proportional extent, our life's decisions will succeed or fail.

There seems to be another truth in the scheme of these things. That is the state of being in love or devotion. It translates into the intensity with which we desire something or somebody. If the intensity of desire is overwhelmingly strong, then it will cause God to act in favor of that desire and make it come true, notwithstanding the 'wrongness' of the desire due to an incomplete knowing of our conscience. It would appear that state of being in love is a state well beyond the state of being right or wrong.

Thus, there are two paths to ensuring that our desires are fulfilled. One is via the complete understanding of our conscience. This is a gradual analytical process that allows our conscience to become representative of our God; and thus, making the desire of our conscience the same as the will of God, which must, therefore, be fulfilled. The second path is via acquiring a state of being in Love whereby a man desires something so intensely that God decides to act on his behalf, and the desire is successful.

People involved in the fulfillment of desire play their role; each, by acting on their conscience independently of one another. It is up to God to align these various acts of the consciences in harmony towards success. That is the dominion of God and only God. God will perform this function irrespective of whether the man believes in God or not. God is needed for this function. Man cannot perform this function, and attempts by man to perform this function will lead to anxiety and pain.

A man acts his conscience. That is it; it ends there; there is no place to be anxious about the results.

This is the vision with which I woke up. During the hours of sleepiness and wakefulness my mind struggled with these questions, and the answers came in that process.

*

I sat in front of the central church park, around 10 am[29]. I allowed my thoughts to drift. And a type of sleepiness came over me, and my mind started working like it was during the night after smoking. I guess some residual effect of marijuana remains.

It seems that the mind and thoughts are sharp during this experience of a smoking episode. However, the mind works much the same way as it is used to working under normal situations. For example, it will continue to be analytical, heuristic, artistic, sexual, if it normally is so. Further, the mind during the episodes does not seem to bring new thoughts, it gets its clues from what had been happening, or what happens during "witnessing experience" episodes. It sees things happen. The happenings are often not sharp but dream like, but the mind is sharp and quick to resolve any questions that arise during the episode. All questions get resolved, for all situations. The resolution is completely satisfactory to the mind in that state, at that time. After waking up, the same explanation might be difficult to recall, and if we can recall some, it might not seem acceptable. That is largely because the detailed clarity of the situation is gone after waking up. In other words, the mind perceives the same happenings differently while awake and during the

---

[29] San Pedro de la Laguna, Guatemala: Wednesday December 7, 2011.

influence of marijuana. The difference seems to arise from the fact that all things are clearer to the mind while under the influence; the way the events are interrelated and correlated, and the reasons behind such relations: such understanding is lost after waking up.

Mushrooms

Got up around 9 am, had herbal tea and two slices with honey[30]. Talked to Elli about the mushrooms that they had brought the day before, and he said the mushrooms were not the best; he also thought the quantity was not enough. He suggested La Cumbre for mushrooms.

I got the mushrooms from La Cumbre. I thought I will eat them at night. Elli had suggested the mushrooms to be taken in nature; colors and views in nature are great and appear in 3D; though you do not see unicorns. I decided to walk along the San Mateo road and have the mushrooms in nature.

Along the road I met Steve who is staying in San Mateo Rio Hondo, writing his autobiography as a fiction, he calls it Tales of Nashara Shah. He is an Englishman, who as a doctor, volunteers for Union Carbide, in connection with the Bhopal accident; for off and on 40 years. He hitchhiked in 70s from England to Pakistan without a pound in his pocket. He is fluent in Hindi.

He rolled a cigarette with hashish in it and I shared about four puffs with him. Apparently did nothing to me.

I stopped a little after the school, on the right-hand side, where a tiny water stream goes across the road. I sat there and had all seven of

---

[30] San Jose del Pacifico, Mexico: Friday October 20, 2017.

my mushrooms. It did nothing to me, just my walk was a little tipsy, but no 3D views or bright colors. I said to myself what is all the emphasis on mushrooms?

I decided to walk back; I think it was over a mile from the hostel, though going back it was all downhill. As I started walking back, within ten minutes I started feeling sleepy. I sat on a cemented platform and immediately got into a vision. But the property was guarded by dogs; they started barking and I got up and started walking again. To resist sleep and keep walking, it was like holding back a dam of water of sleepy vision. Strange that I did not get hit by a vehicle, but the traffic was light and, somehow, I made it back to the hostel.

I managed to open the door, throw my things on the neighboring bed and dropped dead on my bed. It did not take a millisecond for me to drop into a vision. I felt cold even though the weather was sunny and not windy. I put on my jacket.

The vision was so intense, and not all pleasant. I had heard to eat something if the action gets intense. So, I ate eight small chocolate cookies and drank some water. But it did not make much difference.

I discovered I could get out of the vision if I removed the bed sheets from my head.

It was as if there was this infinity of space in which I slipped into in my vision. There was no time in this infinity, just some waves of color lines flowing and interacting; and there were no entities, just constantly changing wave motion and patterns, like the patterns of constantly changing and complicated intensity magnetic lines of field.

The fields interacted, when the flow shifted to the right the feelings got painful; when the flow shifted to my left the feelings were happy. The shifts were constant and unpredictable. When the feelings became too painful, I could not bear it, it was like diving into hell. When this happened, I managed to interrupt the flow and vision by using my hands to remove the sheets from my face.

During the vision I was totally unaware of my existence, my body, and my body parts. The only evidence of my existence was the feelings I felt. I was unaware of my body, and body parts, but somehow, I could use my hands to get out of the vision of painful flows when it got too intense to bear. Occasionally I would briefly become aware of my feet or my hands. I would look at my hands and realize that I have an existence, but the feeling of existence would soon melt away.

I thought somehow about hell and paradise, which in this vision were shift of the flows to the right or to the left. I thought my karma somehow controlled the shift of these flows.

The vision was that of an infinity, filled with energy waves, with the flows controlled by karma. But this is not entirely true, for within the flows there were no existential entities. In the absence of entities, it is hard to imagine the concept of karma. The existence of my feelings however did indicate my existential entity, and therefore in that context a concept of karma might be experienced[31].

For a while I entertained the idea that the infinity was filled with pure energy with no content of any entity, just uniform flowing energy

---

[31] Note added while editing, May 31, 2023: But again, how would the concept of karma arise without any other existential entity in the vision.

patterns, very dynamic and turbulent at times. The existential entity, I thought, was a quantum foam type effect. So, the existential entities emerge, and emerge like transient phenomenon.

Slowly I started to get out of this infinite energy layer. I would see my hands or realize my breathing and that would tend to momentarily take me out of this energy flow layer. After many such transitions, I left this layer of uniform infinite energy flow.

The next phase had existential entities and causality in it – causality meaning cause and effect relationships. In the previous phase there was no causality, no time. In that phase, the mysterious concept of karma did seem to exist but in a peripheral sort of way.

In this phase with existential entities, the concept of causality seemed to show up naturally. Of course, there can be no concept of causality if all that exists is an infinite energy flow without interacting existential entities.

In the entities-causality phase I had entered into the region of complete and perfect transparency, in the sense that any question about the world that occurred to me, its explanation and answer was immediately available with perfect clarity and complete satisfaction. There were no unanswered questions. I think that this phase was demonstrated to me in San Pedro La Laguna. However, the more fundamental layer of infinite energy flows did not exist in that experiential demonstration in San Pedro La Laguna.

I would ask a question and look at the answer and explanation and laugh at the absurdity of the picture that emerged from that explanation.

I think I was in the infinite energy phase and the transparency phase for roughly the same amount of time. But getting out of the infinite energy phase was like waking up to the world of my existence such as a deep breath or looking at my fingers or feeling my feet. Getting out of the transparency phase was more complex. I would ask questions look at the answers, contemplate on the relationships and corollaries and be amused at certain unneeded phenomenon or the absurdity of certain actions and behaviors. I would keep doing it and getting amused.

What almost dragged me out was the receptionist (owner) talking on the phone in somewhat panicky voice, rushing down the wooden stairs, starting his car and leaving, and returning in few minutes.

Even then I did not leave the transparency phase.

I demanded that something must happen that tells me to leave the transparency phase. And that happened momentarily.

It dawned on me how much and how intensely and how unconditionally One Existence loves us. Like a parent, both like a mother and like a father. I thought about my own father and mother. How they took care of me with loving devotion, even when I misbehaved. How I did not value their love. How I behaved in a way that hurt them deeply. How it did not affect their love for me even an epsilon.

One Existence loves me and will provide for me. This love and provisions are for me even if I do nothing to deserve it.

If this is so, why do I need degrees and jobs and all the peripherals? They are irrelevant. Just like a child is loved and cared for by the parents, without the child qualifying for any of it, everyone is loved and cared for without needing to possess any qualifying traits. All I have to do is take this love of One Existence and enjoy it; not even necessarily be thankful for it, or even after being hurtful in my behavior – One Existence's love and caring is not affected.

All I have to do to be happy and fulfilled is to spread the love that I receive from One Existence. Any loving of mine is for my own happiness, otherwise One Existence will give infinite love to everyone, anyway.

Having realized this, I felt no need to become smart by knowing the cause-and-effect relationships. So, I willingly left the transparency phase. I was filled with love from One Existence.

I got up, went to the toilet. I sat down on the veranda chair waiting for water to heat for my shower. The sun was giving its cheerful light and comforting warmth. The clouds were hanging on the ground and up. The trees were smiling at me. The world was full of bountiful love. With intense happiness I went to take shower.

As I came out of the shower Samantha was waiting for me. Some French kids had given her free mushrooms. She was happy too with mushrooms. It was such perfect timing to enhance my happiness, all engineered by One Existence. I told her about my mushroom experience. She listened on. I had not eaten the whole day. I was not feeling hungry but wanted to eat. She suggested we go to La Cumbre, watch the sunset there, and eat a Ralyuda. We did go there, I saw her place, and met her boyfriend. From the restaurant it was a splendid sunset view. While Ralyuda was cooking she went to her place and made a pot of wonderful tea with Mezcal, served in a coconut shell. Then she went to sleep. I returned and wrote down this account.

I am so happy for this day.

*

I feel[32] I do not know how to translate my visions: my vision of the phase of Infinite Energy Flows; my vision of causal phenomena that were demonstrated in the phase of Transparency; and my vision of the phase of One Existence's infinite and unconditional love.

The first vision uses the energy pattern flows in an infinite space with no concept of time in it and without existential entities in it. The second vision uses existential entities in it and the concept of time and causality: these concepts were absent in the first vision. The third vision uses the One Existence and his infinite and unconditional love, forgiveness like that of the parents towards an infant, without judgement of the people like the parents do not judge an infant, without expectation of anything from the people like the parents do not expect anything from the infant, and with no requirement from the people to qualify for this love (unconditional love).

Each vision uses unique constructs that are missing in the other two visions. So, they are completely independent visions, independent of one another. They are perhaps complimentary visions; that is why they were shown to me one after another.

---

[32] This and the following three paragraphs were added while editing on May 31, 2023.

Because each vision uses unique constructs that are not used in the other two, they cannot be translated into one another. But can they be combined into one larger vision?

This is the next day[33].

I feel I do not know how to translate my vision of the phase of Infinite Energy Flows into causal phenomena that were demonstrated in the phase of Transparency, or either one of them into the phase of One Existence's infinite and unconditional love.

The three phases seem to exist without interfaces that can be clearly inferred.

This morning I realized I might be misunderstanding One Existence's love when I said what is the need for degrees and jobs. One Existence will love us and nourish us unconditionally; however, we need to know how to appreciate, receive and benefit from this love and nourishing. Some ways will make us happy and fulfilled and others will not. I mentioned above one such way, namely to spread the love we receive from One Existence.

Nothing is explicitly changed in my current theory of spirituality. That is because this theory lives in the phase of Transparency, and that had already been demonstrated to me in San Pedro La Laguna.

The new work may be to incorporate the new phase of Infinite Flowing Energy because that is the new experiential vision in this new demonstration in San Jose del Pacifico.

---

[33] San Jos del Pacifico, Mexico: The next day to Mushrooms, Saturday, October 21, 2017,

And the matter of One Existence's love that seemed to make me indifferent to the transparency phase needs to be further understood. Maybe, I need another vision somewhere sometime. Each vision will probably necessitate yet another vision because infinity cannot be exhausted.

Today I will go to San Mateo and I will talk to Steve about it.

*

May be a week back or so, I realized this point[34]. However, I did not write it down till now.

I had realized during my vision this point about the flow of infinite energy going right or going left. When it went to the right, it created such intense pain and horror. That happened very quickly as soon as the flow started moving towards the right; and the intensity of pain grew faster than exponential, actually even faster. I did not experience the intensity and horror during the vision because as soon as it started happening, I just could not take it and I interrupted it by using my hand to uncover my face.

During the vision I had explicitly thought and asked where does this flow towards the right that was so horrible and intensely painful, where does it reach? What had occurred to me is this: it is the entry into hell. The words of Quran to describe Hell are too lenient to describe this experience that I had. And it was an experience that involved no fire; the pain and horror just happened; and grew faster than

---

[34] San Jose del Pacifico, Mexico: Friday, November 10th, 2017.

exponential; and that, as I recall, I could not bear it more than few seconds.

During the vision I asked where does this flow lead to? It seemed to me that it was leading to utter death, complete annihilation of the person, complete extinction. It could be the end! Somehow it occurred to me during the vision that it was leading to a new birth. And during the vision, I recalled the Quranic verse: Khalaqal Mauta Wal Hayata[35]. It seemed to fit in so well and I marveled at it. We first Die in the fashion of my vision, and then we are born Alive? I marveled at Quran mentioning Death before Life!

When the flow moved towards the left, it was pleasant, soothing, and no worry kind of state. However, it never became ecstatic. It never went into the depth to give me a demonstration of Paradise if that is what the experience represented. On the contrary, the movement towards the right, it seems to me, provided me an in-depth experience about Hell, assuming that is what it represented.

---

[35] He created death and life. (Quran 67:2)

Follow the Conscience

I was thinking that I cannot be travelling forever[36]. And I recalled some projects that I could do, including three that I had picked up during this travel in Oaxaca.

But I soon realized that the projects can become a distraction from following my real enquiry. The real question for me at a personal level is to discover things like the following. What do I want? What do I want to do with my life? How to free myself from attachments?

These are hard questions to answer. Often, instead of addressing the hard questions, we are distracted by undertaking projects. These mostly are in the form of helping others, the needy and less fortunate. Such humanitarian projects are a common attraction dangled before us by religions and societies; telling us that the real happiness lies in helping others; and helping others is somehow a noble thing to do. Instead of working to eliminate poverty, the idea of humanitarian projects pacifies us. It saves us from feeling bored, and keeps us from going into activism which could challenge the society.

For example, charities are established by the rich, and doing so uses the poverty of others to feel good about themselves and feel superior and fortunate for having acquired riches, enabling them to become the

---

[36] San Jose del Pacifico, Mexico: Wednesday, November 11th, 2017.

upper hand. It is one way the religion and the society reenforce the value it attaches to riches. Instead, we must challenge the society towards egalitarian and just ways that would help eliminate the need for charities. Everyone must have equal opportunity for self-discovery and self-realization.

The future is like the flow of a river: it finds its own path, also in unexpected situations and in unexpected ways. Future is ours to see unfold in front of our very eyes.

*

Like the river, I must remain 'on the move'[37]. However, that means dynamism, not just physical travel. The river must always flow, which indicates its dynamism. Also, the river must leave itself to the workings of gravity, so that it can flow effortlessly and joyfully. For example, the river does not see or foresee the rocks and boulders, canyons and mountains in its path; it does not worry about dealing with those things, it just flows under gravity and gravity takes care of 'how to deal with it'. This type of effortless and joyful flow will grow flowers in the valley of the river, produce rainbows in its white foam, and produce songs that never stop.

Again, the river does not know or care for these flowers, rainbows, and songs – they just happen without the river being aware of them or intending them. The 'harmony' of Nature takes care of the flowers, rainbows, and songs.

---

[37] San Jose del Pacifico, Mexico: Sunday, November 12th, 2017.

In human life, I think the gravity is replaced by One Existence which is hidden in the 'desire' for 'self-discovery'. However, it does not imply an awareness of One Existence, far that it would mean a belief in it. It merely requires a childlike unstoppable desire to 'self-discover'. And to stay away from things that stand in the way of this desire. If so, one can march ahead with this desire, without a need to prepare for dealing with what is coming ahead. We live every moment, we know our spiritual way, and the "way" will connect the moments. There is no room for fear of the unknown, and anxiety about uncertainty. Let the "way" connect the dots; let the conscience show us this "way" and keep us on it. This type of "living" expands life into the domain of conscience which is the same thing as the 'inner-self'. The inner self takes care of the causality for the traveler along the "spiritual way", just as the gravity takes care of the flow for a river without the river knowing what gravity is, or what it will do for its flow. We travel along the "spiritual way" by using our innate capabilities: senses, intellect, and conscience. Where the senses and the intellect leave gaps, we trust those gaps to the care of our conscience. This is how we go into meta-science; this is how we gradually enter the domain of Ishq: the Sufi way to self-discover.

I am not sure if I am in the domain of Ishq; but I am certainly bumbling around knocking at the boundary between science and Ishq. Iqbal illustrates this boundary in this verse:

be-khatar kuud paḌā ātish-e-namrūd meñ ishq

aql hai mahv-e-tamāshā-e-lab-e-bām abhī[38]

I believe that self-discovery is the only way to live one's life; it is also the very purpose of life. I cannot run away from this realization, because I seem to have internalized it. This situation can produce contradictions in life. For example, I always was critical of Buddha for leaving his wife behind and going on the journey for self-discovery. Now, I am sort of doing similar myself. I have tried to go many times, and given it up each time; I guess for the same reasons that I was critical of Buddha. Perhaps this is how the domain of rationality pulls us back into itself and stops us from crossing the boundary into "Ishq". Training in rationality, like mine in theoretical physics, becomes a baggage for crossing into the domain of Ishq. It seems that Buddha might eventually have crossed this boundary; and he was able to take a sudden and final leap into Ishq. He might have thanked the fact that he was not a theoretical physicist like myself.

So far, I am finding the process of self-discovery effortless and joyful; having no anxiety of what will happen to me; having no fear of failure, and having no anxiousness for success.

*

---

[38] While Ishq knows and, to please the beloved, jumps into the trial situation in a wink, the intellect is still standing by the wayside and busy in contemplation.

At night while going to sleep, it occurred to me what it means to leave things to "conscience"; just to follow the heart and go on the journey of self-discovery, carefree and joyously[39]. But how does "conscience" know how to take care of us, and guide us correctly?

My revelation is that the conscience knows it through having witnessed the experiential-manifestations of it. It is the "knowing" via the other means than the "scientific" means. It is the alternative way of finding out, different than the scientific rational and analytic means. These experiential-manifestations that the conscience invokes are like having an explicit dream ahead of an event actually taking place. It is like watching a movie about something happening, before it actually happens. The conscience knows it ahead of time, it can guide us in ways that we cannot guide ourselves using rational and analytic means, which are the only means that we have at our disposal if we do not listen to the conscience.

The two means of knowing are not that different though their scopes and techniques are very different. The analytic means can extrapolate data to know the future. For example, we have weather forecasts, hour by hour information, day by day weather, and long-term climatic projections. Our conscience can do that too, and predict the future through experiential manifestations. What is the nature and mechanism of these experiential manifestations? It is not clear to me at this time. Perhaps one difference is the time variable: time exists in a very central manner in science, and it perhaps does not exist in the ways

---

[39] San Jose del Pacifico, Mexico: Monday, November 13th, 2017.

of the conscience. In the conscience, therefore, a totality of all time-series exists simultaneously; it exists as overlays of knowledge on a map of events, yet to be defined in detail[40].

Scientific means are by definition probabilities and can be in error in their extrapolations and predictions. Does the conscience make similar mistakes in its predictions, just as the weather analysis is sometimes in error? At this stage it is not clear to me. Perhaps the conscience does not make mistakes because it is connected to the totality of the world in a non-probabilistic way. The two, working within their own scopes, cannot contradict each other and must agree within their common sphere of validity. This is so because of the Equivalence Principle: the workings through physicality and the workings through spirituality are equivalent.

---

[40] Note: The journey of self-discovery is a very long one, and the matters of "Ishq" enter into this journey at advanced stages. Some content of this discourse apply only for the travelers in advanced stage; the vast majority who have only barely begun should strictly adhere to rationality and scientific approaches. That is because the human conscience gets buried underneath the externally induced values and indoctrinations. Even though the conscience always knows, its voice is not audible when it is buried deep underneath; or when it does become audible, it is invariably so muffled up that it is not possible to clearly understand it, while the conscience is still buried deep underneath. Much of the journey is spent in minimally discovering one's own conscience; and that requires long years of hard work to remove the heaps of externally induced values and indoctrinations.

CBD Candy

Yesterday around 10:30 Am I took a candy with 20 mg of Cannabis, mainly just CBD[41]. Within about 20 minutes I started to feel sleepy. I slept on the sofa for about 30 minutes; then went to the bathroom, and went to sleep in my bed.

I was only vaguely conscious of my surroundings. I remember someone coming and using the bathroom; do not remember any voice. It was like lying there with an empty mind; a mind that did not think or contemplate, though it still observed. Its emptiness was demonstrated to me. At a moment I would clearly read and understand as if from a memory location, shown to me as a continuum of bits and bytes. The very next moment I tried to read the same memory, but I could not read it, nor could I recall what I had read from the same memory location just a moment earlier. Sort of a display of a volatile memory.

It did not concern me that I could not read the content. And it did not concern me when I could read those content. The result did not matter. The effort did not matter. I sought no meaning in the content when I could read it, and I sought no meaning in the content when I could not read them. The meaning itself was of no meaning or

---

[41] Bowie, MD: Thursday, December 10, 2020.

consequence. Though I remember thinking that it was a demonstration of a volatile memory.

After a while I started feeling less empty minded. I recall thinking about something, and then thinking what effect that thing in my life has on the memory of myself after I go. I vividly recall realizing that this concern about one's legacy is just a reflection of ego; and how such a concern is not natural but a concern that is planted within us by our society; just as religion plants within us the questions like the purpose of life, who created us and for what purpose? So, this question that our ego concerns itself regarding our legacy is an artificially planted concern coming from indoctrination by our society in the form of national heroes and human icons.

After that my wife entered and tried to wake me up, but I did not wake up. I recall she was concerned but not too much. She took my BP and Sugar which were normal. She speculated why I was so, and my son who was right there did not mention about me taking cannabis. She went out closing the bedroom door to let me sleep on.

After about half an hour I was up with my eyes open. But I was still not 'thinking'; I was just alert with a pseudo empty mind. She returned and then I told her about cannabis; she was relieved knowing that the effect will wain with time. And then there was Azaan. I was thinking it was around 2PM but it was Maghrib Azaan at 4:45 PM.

It was similar experience in San Pedro la Laguna; it had lasted from about 11am to 5 pm. But that was with marijuana; and this was just CBD with supposedly no THC.

Observations

Community

What I say is valid[42]. However, it is so within a context. The contexts can be different. The context is something we do not enunciate explicitly; rather, we assume it. This works when we all come from the same or similar communities. However, when we come from different communities, we are used to different meanings and protocols for doing things that are familiar to all within the community. But the cultures, thoughts, and societal assumptions are different in different communities.

I am happy living in the community that I am in by fate. I thank the powers above for this kindness. However, are most people happy living in the community they are in by fate?

Let us appreciate the difference between being comfortable and being happy. Comforts can be individual, largely based on the community attitudes. But happiness is more universal. Comforts originate from external sources, while the happiness originates from within.

There are three groups in USA. The so called 1% and 99%. The 99% of the people live on one tenth of the national wealth, while the 1% enjoy the rest of the national wealth. There are further two groups among the 99%, those below the subsistence level and those above it.

---

[42] Bowie, MD: August 11, 2014.

Those below the subsistence level are roughly one tenth; about 40 million citizens. That is how USA is as a community.

Even those people above the subsistence level are living a hard life. They work multiple jobs. Both spouses often work. Under the pressure of the economic inequity within the community, children are left without parental love a good part of the day. Family structure is under tension, and often at breaking point. Majority of US people are above the desperation level, but they are not comfortable, and they are not happy.

On the other hand, the life of most folks in the Mayan community of Mexico is not comfortable; though many of them are happy. Pursuit of happiness is what life of a person seeks within a community.

Happiness is rather universal; it is not individualistic. We cannot be happy without our spouses being happy; we cannot be happy without our families being happy; our families cannot be happy without our community being happy. A community cannot be happy with its substantial population being unhappy.

The poor people are struggling worldwide. Most work but get very little for their work. Despite their struggles they are getting poorer, and more and more people are becoming poor. If people want to be happy, we need to do something about it. The rich people are fast becoming richer. Government loopholes are deliberately created and maintained, worldwide, to make the rich people richer at the expense of the poor people. As the rich people grow richer, they also grow in their clout, and more loopholes are created to serve them; thereby making the poor people poorer. Most communities have become places for the rich, where the poor people carry greater and greater burden. We need to do something about it to make the world a happy community.

All this is happening perfectly legally. The fruits of this legal system are bitter. Justice has served the rich but has betrayed the poor. We need to do something about it. What can we do about it? To reform the evil using evil? To fight a corrupt system with money? At the same time, it seems to me that the worldwide system is corrupt; democratic representation and the government of the people, by the people, and for the people, are mere pretenses.

The worldwide community has become corrupt and it is acting unjustly to its members. What is the scope for repairing this corruption, and the scope for changing the injustice into a commitment to caring?

Our community mission is to change a greedy culture into a spiritual living, where everyone is happy, according to his or her own idea of happiness; not a sterile static happiness but one that is dynamic and grows to envelop all. This requires a community that is different than the worldwide community that exists today.

Individual and Community

I have been thinking this thought over past few days, less than a week; expressed in this translation of a Rumi poem[43]:

> Now is the time to know
> That all that you do is sacred.
> Now, why not consider
> A lasting truce with yourself and God.
> Now is the time to understand
> That all your ideas of right and wrong
> Were just a child's training wheels;
> To be laid aside
> When you can finally live
> With veracity,
> And love.
> My dear, please tell me,
> Why do you still
> Throw sticks at your heart
> And God?

---

[43] Iran: Friday, March 28, 2014.

What is it in that sweet voice inside

That incites you to fear?

Now is the time for the world to know

That every thought and action is sacred.

This is the time

For you to deeply compute the impossibility

That there is anything

But Grace.

This thing is stuck with me, as if I knew it all along and Rumi gave it an expression.

Life is sacred. That is so in the sense that everything that a living being does is sacred. It is sacred despite often times the appearance of things. Is it sacred what Hitler did in Europe; is it sacred what Bush did in Iraq? The answer is yes despite the uncomfortable feelings it brings, despite the conflict it invokes. What uncomfortable feelings? What conflict with what? The sweet voice inside says it is all sacred because the act of living is sacred. Then our ideas about right and wrong incite a fear within us. No, what Hitler did cannot be sacred; no, what Bush did cannot be sacred. There is a latent fear about what we regard to be right and wrong, and someone or some situation will challenge those ideas of ours; our ideas about that we want to hold about right and wrong. This fear to let go of the ideas is interfering with the sacredness of living. Let go of the training wheels, and learn to deeply compute the impossibility that there is anything but Grace.

So let go of the ideas of yours that you regard as self-evident with respect to things being right and wrong. You let go of those ideas because they stand in your act of living a life, your own life. You let go of these ideas not because they have ceased to function, but because you have moved on to reach new states where the functions that these ideas serve have themselves become redundant. You want to ride freely on the open roads; the training wheels are only a hindrance in that open and free ride.

The ideas about right and wrong are the training wheels on the road to an open and free life. Let go of them. Take them off and put them aside. They are now only a hindrance in your way; assuming you have reached that far along the "way".

Still, you are afraid to let go of those notions of right and wrong. Don't worry, there is no hurry. Do it when you feel the self-evidence for doing so; if you see it, when you see it. Do not let them go before you cease to have a need for them. Things cannot be hurried; they cannot happen before their time. If you are afraid to let go of the training wheels, by all means keep them. We are all here to live our life, and to live it well. There is nothing to worry about. Life is sacred; whether it is lived with training wheels or without them. But keep the training wheels only because you know they serve a good function for you. Do not hold on to the training wheels because you have managed to incite fear in the sacred melody of life. If it is the fear, then it is time to know that life is all grace; there is no place in it for fear. Always remember this for a metaphor: you will not enjoy the free and smooth ride to the wide and open spaces till you let go of the training wheels.

Residents and Wanderers

Since Christmas day I have been sick[44]. Started with common cold, but had slight temperature which made it much worse for me. I spent most of the 5 days in bed. Felt chills, mild body aches. Could not sit on the sofa for an hour without getting tired and going back to bed. On Dec 30 went to doctor; this cold is something going around, he said.

Next day it felt so renewing to sit on the sofa normally. I could take a shower that felt like a reassuring experience; and to listen to the music on the shower radio felt refreshing. Just five days of deprivation of these things gave them a new meaning in my life. Things it seems mean different things depending upon our own disposition.

*

I was looking out of the kitchen window in Adnan's apartment in Istanbul[45]. I saw the washed clothes on the clothes line. That gave me the perception that these people live here for their lives, while we are just passing through in transit. I asked Adnan what he thought the difference was between people who live at a place and those who pass through the place in transient mode. His reply was very thorough and

---

[44] Bowie, MD: January 1st, 2015.

[45] Istanbul, Turkey: Monday, March 23rd, 2015.

objective. I do not know if I can recapture it here. This is what I can recall now.

People who live at a place take their situations seriously, because they have to work to change their situation. Those in transit can just live it out for a period without the necessity to have to change the situation. The situation will pass for them whatever attitude they adopt towards it; meaning whatever it is it is not there to stay, for when they move on, they will not need to deal with it.

There are things that impact the residents in essential ways, such as job situation, economy, and quality of health care. For the transient folks these things do not matter for they do not seek a job, they bring their money from outside, and if a health situation arises, they can afford to pay or go back.

People who live at a place need to pay attention to social matters and society norms because they have to be there for a long time. They cannot be social outcasts, and they cannot afford to be on the wrong side of influential people. For those passing in transit, the social norms are a diversity to observe and enjoy, and the influential people have no influence over them because the transient people do not require the services and resources which the influential people can control.

Then I asked what effect it has on someone who is always in a transit mode. Again, Adnan was insightful and thorough. I am not sure what he said. But it included this. Such a person would not be able to have close friends. He said for himself, even if he does not see his friends for a long time, when they do meet, they connect naturally and effortlessly, as if they had not been away from each other. On the other hand, when I look at myself, I do not have any such friends, because in addition to my travels, I have migrated at least seven times, which have had an uprooting effect; and loss of my friends.

Truth and the Filters

I have been going around in Iran since March 6; now 18 days[46]. I see these people; friendly, innocent, curious. To my mortal perception they seem under some pressure, for I find them rarely bubbly, spontaneous, or just being there in the present. I watched women, most did not strike as beautiful. I seem to find grace in women who are among old women of more than middle age. The others seem in some sort of pressure, subdued, not cheerful.

Is it their dress? I do not think so. I find young women who are fashionable, so to speak, and they are especially not attractive; there seems some sort of artificiality in them, as if they are not comfortable with themselves. I see men also are not spontaneous, not lively, bubbly. They are rather serious, thoughtful.

In Tehran some had complained about USA. In Esfahan a sweet young kid had talked about 8 years of war with Iraq, saying Saddam was really a bad man. In Qom I visited their counterpart of the Arlington Cemetery; 200,000 Shohada of Iraq war.

It seems the war has left the nation with scars. It seems USA has created a real resentment among people, a sort of resentment that comes from long lived suffering, unjustified suffering, a sort of oppression.

---

[46] Iran: Sunday, March 23rd, 2014.

This seems to be the sentiment in Iran when people talk about USA. A taxi driver (I forget where, perhaps in Tehran) told me "we are free, we do what we want".

Things have to be understood in their context and prospect. That helps understand how things are and how things appear to us. This struck me particularly at three different occasions.

First it was in Naqshe Jehan Hotel in Tehran. It is on a busy street, Chahar Bagh Payin. I think that was the day I was not feeling well, sort of felt as if I had had a kind of transient stroke during the night before; my left leg felt weak. I took a Nitroglycerine; I do not remember what time.

I sat in the lobby, a nominal lobby with a table and four chairs. The hotel door was closed; it had double doors; both were closed. No noise was coming in. It was comfortably warm inside. I may have been having tea, but I am not sure. I thought to myself: if I was always in this lobby, never stepped out, would I know the hustle and bustle, the traffic that goes on, on the street, outside? I could see some passersby in the street, passing in front of the glass door quietly; and I could see the vehicles pass in the closest lane, again quietly (because no noise was coming in). Could I ever understand what really happens outside on the street from these silent glimpses? If I always lived in the lobby and never stepped out, what would be my reality about what goes on in the street? Now let me step out and observe what happens on the street. I see the hustle and bustle, the mad traffic, the shops, the trees that line both sides on the boulevard. That would be my new reality. But is that the true reality of the street, or just my perception of it?

We often label as the true reality, what we all agree that it is what happens. So, what I perceive as the reality about the street may be perceived as truly 'the reality of the street'. The true reality is the collective perception about a situation by a community of people. Interesting things can happen when this true perception that prevails in a society is challenged, and an alternative to that truth emerges. We live according to our truths; a little change in the set of our truths causes a big change in our attitude about life, our own life.

Second time it happened in Shiraz when I was in the Amir Khan Castle. It is not a big castle, nothing compared with Mughal castles in Lahore, Delhi, or Agra. The middle part just has trees which they call Chaman. The boundary walls have some rooms and exhibits. In the middle is a long reflection pool; seems to be a common thing in Iranian historical buildings, palaces, mosques, and now a castle.

It was Nau Roz so there were lot of people, families with children. They were busy taking pictures, women posing near the pool and among trees. And then I went inside a room near where a display with wax statues is shown, a replica of a meeting room Karim Khan. I could see through the glass door, but no sounds were coming. Suddenly it was hard to make sense of the movements of the people; it placed me somewhat in a detached situation. As an observer I was somewhat detached from the situation being observed because of the sound barrier.

Third time it happened was in the central courtyard of the Neyazesh Hotel in Shiraz. It is a nice restaurant where we have breakfast (included with the room, dorm in my case); and we can also have dinner here. When it is sunny, the light comes through plastic covers at the peripheral of the high atrium; these covers can be raised or dropped. Most of the atrium is fixed with blue, but the peripheral blinds have an orange tinge. When I am there during the breakfast or just sitting around the day, the letters on the screen of my phone look sharp orange. Are they orange or black? Made me aware of the filtering process that goes on in what we call observations. What are the filtering processes that are always present during all observations? Those determine the environment of our observations; environment that we may not even be aware of its nature, because of the filters that it contains and always applies. How do we allow for filters that we do not even know that they exist?

So, what is our reality? That depends on three things: us as observers; phenomena that are observed; and the invisible filters that are integral part of the environment in which the observer lives and the phenomena take place. What then is our reality? What is our environment? What are we in the capacity of observers? What are the phenomena that we decide we want to observe, or they make their presence felt to us in our environment so that we decide to make an effort to observe them? The reality depends upon all of these, and others that we may not be aware of.

The truth about the reality is merely the name of the consensus that may emerge within all observers in a society. Such a consensus may even be contrived using the conditioning that the forces in the society are capable of applying upon the individuals in the society.

So, is there a reality? Is there a truth? Perhaps not!

When I travel around the world, I do not just go to the monuments and the wonders of the world. I go to small places. I observe people. I observe life as it flows in streets, cities, and towns. Here in Iran, I observed that when normal life is interrupted under unbearable external forces, life is disconnected from its natural cheerfulness and flow.

Human Behavior

Early morning around 4 am I put off the lights in the living room and opened the curtains[47]. There was street light outside, some porch lights on the neighboring houses, and some dim porch lights from the far end of the loop. There was only one star I could see through the big wide window.

I thought to myself so and so lives in that house. And then I thought does he still live in that house when he is out at work? Is that porch light still his when he is not at home? Is the house still his when he is away on vacation? And I asked similar questions about myself. Was this house still mine when I was out walking to my hotel on a road in Turkey?

The answer is that things are ours only for a duration of time. When the durations are long, like 10 years, we assume the posture that we own those things. So, we own our home, we own our car, and we have our job. When the duration is small like few minutes, we use a different terminology. We say things like this seat is mine, it is my turn, this is my location in the queue. It is only a matter of time when that position in the queue will not be mine, I will not own that car, and that house will no longer be mine. The ownership and possession of things

---

[47] Bowie, MD: August 15-16, 2014.

is all temporary. Beyond that time, we possess nothing and we own nothing.

That reminded me of the Punjabi saying: jehra kha leya te handa leya uuhi apna ai. (we own only what we have eaten and digested, and what we have worn and worn out). And then I wondered at the effectiveness of that saying. Why it is so agreeable? It is because of two things. It is expressed using words that people abundantly use all the time. And it is talking about actions that everyone does for basic survival, and does them frequently, on daily basis. Despite all that effectiveness, spontaneity of the language, and the homeliness of the experience – despite all that agreement with the truth of the statement, people nevertheless live as if it were not true. People strive at ownership, people hoard and accumulate more than they need, and people live as if life is permanent. Why there is this dichotomy, why there is this gasping divide between the reality that we recognize as valid and true and the persistent and insistent behavior that is contrary to that truth?

Man's behavior it seems is not governed by what he knows to be true, rather it is governed by the imitation of what he finds everyone else around him to be doing. When a truth that he knows contradicts the mass behavior of the people around him, and he knows that the truth will not benefit him or hurt him in the present time or the immediate future, then he behaves according to the actual conduct of the masses around him rather than according to the truth that he knows. Further, he does not imitate the majority around him; rather, he imitates and emulates a minority of the people whom he admires and idealizes, like the celebrities and the rich and famous. He acquires this admiration from the indoctrination by the society; the celebration, medals, and awards bestowed upon the designated heroes of the society.

On the other hand, man defends his country and his religion, and he even gladly goes into martyrdom. He does this even though the celebrities do not generally do it, and the rich and famous do not generally do it.

So, man's behavior is not according to what he knows to be true, unless this truth translates into a benefit or threat of a harm to him at the present time or in the immediate future. Abstract truth does not influence man's behavior unless it translates into some consequences for him in terms of a benefit that would attract him or a harm that would make him afraid. He is led into the behavior that enables him to emulate those he admires and idealizes, namely the legendary heroes of the society, the celebrities, and the rich and famous. When a man seeks martyrdom for reasons of patriotism and the truth of his religion, in reality he is not doing that for either patriotism or religion. It is again the indoctrination by the society. All his life the society tells him how glorified are the martyrs, the saints, the kings, the mythological figures like the Prophets and the avatars, etc.

This is the process of indoctrination of man by the society. A common man finds it out of his reach to become a Prophet, a saint, or a mythical figure. The only thing that he finds attainable, and the only thing he knows how to attain it, is the martyrdom. So, when it comes to a war, it is only the common man who seeks martyrdom because of the indoctrination, and because of it being within his capacity to achieve.

It seems that indoctrination wins over truth for most people. And why is it so? The indoctrination works because it is presented to man by the society as the truth. Now man knows the truth that everything in life is temporary, yet man lives his life as if the things in life are not temporary. Why it is the case that the truth that is so self-evident does not decide man's conduct, while the truth that is presented to man via the societal indoctrination does decide man's conduct? The difference is that the self-evident truth is limited to knowledge of it being the truth, it is not constantly reinforced either in man's experience of his own life or in the practices of the society. On the other hand, the 'truth' that the indoctrination impacts on man is constantly reinforced in the daily life of man's own living as well as in the daily affairs of the society. That is so even if the truth being presented via the indoctrination be actually false, unless its falsehood becomes common knowledge.

It seems that man's daily experience and his observations of the society take precedence and preference in deciding man's behavior in comparison to his abstract knowledge of something being the truth, if it does not translate into some tangible benefit or loss. Man's notion of truth, it would seem, is therefore utilitarian, and it is the utility aspect of the truth that decides man's conduct. Just the utility of something will not necessarily attract man; it must at the same time also be the truth, even if the truth be unverified, a make belief thing, or a mere orchestration by the society.

So, man does care for truth. However, man does not seem to be predisposed for making efforts to verify the truth, which predisposes man to societal indoctrinations. Man's conduct will be impacted by his belief about the truth if and only if his belief about something being the truth translates into tangible benefits and losses in his own life. That is why the society rewards people for upholding the truth that it indoctrinates. A truth will fail to impact man's conduct if the consequences of that truth are not clear to him in the daily life. That is why the truth discovered by Galileo about the motion of the Earth did not attract people; the writ of the Church prevailed even though it was falsehood.

Ask Questions

I got up around 3:30 am, made some tea, ate left over samosa[48]. I opened the blinds fully, sat on the computer chair, looking outside.

I thought about Sardar, how he does not want the car anymore; I thought about Selden, how he did not renew my contract, and how his own contract was not renewed the year after; and I thought about the guy in Iran, how I stayed in his apartment; etc.

I asked myself how my thoughts are jumping around, apparently in a random way. But is it random or is it that a mechanism is driving them around; biological mechanism, and my psychology, etc.?

Then I sat on the Sofa and looked out. I looked at the tree, it was silent, no wind, just standing quietly. I asked is it happy? Then I asked is it better for the tree when there is no wind versus when there is gushing wind? I thought no wind is better for the tree, because the wind would blow its flowers away, and break away its branches. But then I thought that the flowers blowing away helps with pollination and spreading of seeds and continuation of the specie. Which is better for the tree? When is the tree happier? The answer we get is based on our own state, it tells us about ourselves, not necessarily about the tree. The

---

[48] Bowie, MD: April 1st, 2022.

tree lives in a larger reality compared to our smaller reality in which we perceive it.

I looked at the sky. It looks like a blue vault to the naked eye. But science tells us that it is just space, and the blue light of the Sun scatters through the atmosphere. So, there is a naked eye view, and there is a wise-eye view.

Then I thought about the people. We think of our happiness, and what is better for us within the small reality that we perceive. Natural disasters happen, wars happen, genocides happen, all sort of fortunes and misfortunes happen. Is that good for us? Is that bad for us?

Our answers are within the limited reality within which we contemplate. The actual reality is larger. The answers we get are based on our perceived reality, and the meanings of those answers are also based on the reality within which they are contemplated.

Take for example the Iraq war or Afghanistan war. Because of those wars, as an auxiliary matter, the Iraqi and Afghani society has evolved. The war became an unplanned stimulus for that evolution. But the same war plundered the cities, destroyed people's livelihoods, and killed the innocent. Is that good? Is that bad?

Good for the society is not the same as the good for the individual! Somebody died in the war; that was bad for him and the aggrieved ones. But the society improved in some way, and that was good for the next generation!

So, was the war good? Was the war bad? And how about the people who lived through the war? Do they go to heaven? Do they go to hell?

Do they still go to the same heaven or hell, had there been no war? Do we go to heaven or hell without regard to if there is war or there is no war? How are things connected? Is the individual salvation connected to the external circumstances of the society at large; and in a global society, upon the world at large? The person who went to heaven or hell in 5th century, would he/she still go to the same place today?

The lives of the people are intrinsically linked to the society they live in. In Physics there is wave motion theory. There is wave velocity, and then there is group velocity. The group velocity is always less, and is a limiting factor. Now an individual lives with his wave velocity and his living is constrained by the group velocity of his society.

That is one reason why people migrate.

If people's lives are so intertwined with the society they live in, can any scripture prescribe a criterion for salvation independent of the society? A realistic scripture can only provide general guidance, without any fixed criterion for salvation. The meaning of a life changes with the society that it is lived in. A life is not a life in isolation and abstraction; rather, it is a life within a society with all its antecedents and precedents.

During this meditation session, I thought in an open way; any question that I thought of, its answer appeared quite spontaneously, and effortlessly.

And I had met a young man, Pepe, in Mazunte, Mexico, who said it is important to ask questions. He ran a pizza restaurant, and he described it as a "platform to ask questions freely". If we do not ask questions, we do not get answers.

.

Dialogue with Kim

Last night talked to Kim till 4 AM about self-discovery[49]. Kim is a high school kid. He thinks that there is nobody who is not engaged in self-discovery. The lowest level of self-discovery will also bring happiness and peace and fulfillment. And may be that is enough for the person. On the other hand, my observation is that most people do not engage in self-discovery. They are busy with the criteria that do not represent their own inner self, but they represent the indoctrinations of the society. Such people cannot be happy and at peace.

So, there is only one way to settle this difference. We conduct an experiment. Maybe we take a survey of all people asking them if they are happy or peaceful. The result should decide if most people engage in self-discovery or they do not.

Kim says that he would have agreed with my position few weeks earlier. But his recent experiences tell him otherwise, namely that most people engage in self-discovery. I think Kim may not have digested fully his recent experiences, and maybe I should wait what his conclusion will be after he has digested his experiences.

---

[49] Sophia, Bulgaria: May16 and 19, 2015.

Later, Kim told me that some weeks after this conversation he suffered from a panic attack. He went through a lengthy treatment. Nevertheless, I still take his stance seriously.

Kim also described two dynamics that are interesting. They are predicted by my theory of spiritual way but not explicitly discussed in the current version (2015).

During the journey of self-discovery, Kim is describing a dynamic scenario whereby there are exaltations, but following the exaltations there are blue periods in which the exaltations disappear and disappointments arise to a point that seems to give a feeling that all is lost.

I interpret this phenomenon as two different dynamics.

The first dynamic is one of the discovery process. The process is an experimentation, a searching, a seeking. Some experiments work giving rise to happiness and some experiments do not work thereby giving rise to sadness. This accounts for cycles of ups and downs. These are relatively common.

The second dynamic entails major exaltations and major disappointments arising from the lifting of veils during the spirals of the spiritual voyage on the "way". These correspond to the distinct stages in the journey when a veil is lifted and a door opens that leads us to the other side of the veil. When we enter a new stage, it is extreme exaltation, an exaltation of a new type, an exaltation that was not yet experienced or imagined.

Each stage, however, eventually ends with disappointment, a letdown, a seeking of the next stage. This happens for two reasons. First, the exaltation that was so exuberating, after a while does not seem so great because the new stage has come with new openings for experiencing the new reality, where everything is new and exalting. Among the new exuberance, the initial exaltation does not seem so special. The expectations are raised and the search continues to new unexplored heights. The higher expectations give rise to disappointments, and just before the next veil lifts, such disappointments bring really blue periods, often long and filled with darkness, where one is feeling the way with extreme difficulties and uncertainties. When the veil is lifted again, that gives the traveler a taste for what can be, what things mean, and how to experience the new reality. Each stage comes with new sense of realities, such that the truth and reality of the previous stage can even lose its validity and meaning. It can feel that the previous stage was just the training wheels for riding in this new one. Therefore, the intense disappointment before the lifting of the veil is a birth pang that gives rise to the next stage of experiencing truth and reality of a bigger exuberance. The loss of the truth and reality of the previous stage can cause extremely bewildering disappointment and wonderment, as if all could have been in vain. This period lasts till the traveler discovers the new reality corresponding to the new stage. When the new reality is arrived at, the sense of loss disappears and new exaltations show.

This will continue during the journey of life throughout; it is a sign that the traveler is making progress and is not content having reached a particular stage.

The travel is illustrated by the motion along a three-dimensional spiral. The motion seems like it is going in a circle. Then suddenly a veil is lifted, and it feels that the circle has been visibly and emotionally expanded. The spiritual way is a spiral path; it gradually expands in its extent, but it visibly expands when a veil is lifted. Each lifting of the veil is like entering a new spiritual state. The spiral continues infinitely expanding.

As we go from stage to stage, the variations that we discussed above become more intense and sometimes bewilderingly so. Closer we are to our true inner self, more doors for experiencing the truth open for us, and we see the truth more closely than before, and we see it deeper and from more perspectives. This brings more intense ecstasies. We also can lose the truth and reality of the previous stage and that loss can also be intense because what we thought was the reality and truth turn out to be not so. This can produce intense emptiness, disillusionment, and wonderments. It gets huger and huger as we go into higher and higher stages.

At some stage the traveler will become familiar with this cycle of exaltations and disillusionments. The traveler will then attain a steady state as if a stage of silence and stillness has arrived. However, this too is only a stage along the "way" and the spiral path continues to grow and expand infinitely.

Time

Yesterday I woke up early around 4 am[50]. Sat there with a cup of Turkish black tea and a spoonful of honey. Closed all lights, and opened the front drapes so street light came in through the vertical blinds. Things inside and outside seemed different in the dark, rather mystic. I looked at the cars on the street, and tried to state that this car belongs to this person. Same with the sleepy quiet houses. Trying to attribute houses to people seemed a bit unrealistic, given that no people were around. Then I thought, what if everyone died? The cars would still be there, the houses will still be there. Even the street light will still be there, at least for few hours, until the generators run out of fuel. And then I thought if another generation inhabited the land after a long time. They would find the cars, the houses, the electricity generators. Then they will try to build a theory about a past civilization.

Then I thought about myself sitting there, with a cup of tea in my hand, and thinking. My thoughts about doing something, about starting my laptop, or looking at my phone, or something. That 'need to do something' I then mapped on our concept of not to waste time; and I thought about what time is, and why it is that we think about not to waste it.

---

[50] Bowie, MD: Tuesday, February 21, 2017.

I thought of time as just something that we mark by doing events in our life. What if we do not do any of the events? Will time still be around?

I thought about my so-called duties. What if I did not do them? What would change in the universe if I did not do them? Perhaps nothing would change, things will go on, on their merry way! What if I die? What would change in the universe? Nothing! Look at Mr. Salim having died. What has changed in that household? Things have gone on; some have gone even 'better' after his death!

What if there were no people on earth? Would that matter? In the scheme of the universe, it would not be noticed. What if Earth itself did not exist? Would that matter? No, it would not matter! Perhaps the planets would make some corrections to their orbits, in the way nature behaves under gravity, and things would go on as 'normal'! What if the entire solar system was not there? It also would not matter at all! What if the Milky way galaxy was not there? Nothing matters! Nature adjusts and goes on. The presence of things is a perturbation on other things; universe goes on with or without this perturbation; showing no preference for the presence or absence of such perturbations.

Things do not matter!

So, if the events that mark time do not matter, does time itself matter?

Time matters in our scientific equations. It matters because it matters as a matter of our axioms that presuppose for time to exist. It matters because we start the scientific research with the explicit axiom that time matters. So, we cannot understand time within that axiomatic framework, for such a framework will always assert that time matters per the foundational axioms of the framework. Science cannot tell us about time using itself as the framework.

If I keep sitting on the sofa doing nothing, would time matter? Time then would not matter because time then would not exist because there are no events to mark time with. We can answer the question whether time matters only when we have annihilated time by dropping the axiom that time matters!

The nature of things cannot be understood within a framework that presupposes them to exist. And in a different framework where these things do not exist, they do not matter! Therefore, things matter when we presuppose them to exist and they do not matter in a framework where they do not exist. Whether something matters or it does not matter is a matter of our perception about the thing. And this perception is defined by our need for the thing to exist or not to exist. Whatever our perception, the universe does not care about it in the least, in the sense that it has no preference for the thing to exist or not to exist.

If we nickname the universe as god, then god does not care, in the least, about our perceptions about god. God is not affected by these perceptions, or god does not have a preference for a perception to exist or not to exist.

Butterflies in Ecstasy

Yesterday around 3 pm, I took my coffee to the creek, and sat on the swing, looking towards the creek[51].

A pair of butterflies over the water caught my attention. They were flying in unison and flying in whirls and patterns, like the whirling dervishes in ecstasy.

They flew together for about a minute. Then I realized it was the preliminaries for coitus. The male tried to climb over the female, and she kept escaping. She would resist, really seemed to resist. The male would take hold of her, climb over her, and she would flutter away, not really escaping, but in a playful sort of way – perhaps knowing what was meant to happen but prolonging it, sort of enhancing the act, increasing the expectations, and making it joyful by making it playful.

He would catch on to her, and she would let him catch on. And when he thought he really had her, she would fly away, not really away, just fly off to a different branch very close by, or fly off to a different leaf on the same branch.

This creativity of the coitus really impressed me, sort of wondering why humans are not so joyful in the enjoyment of the natural act.

---

[51] Bowie, MD: Sunday, June 9, 2019.

Eventually they were on a leaf, the male climbed over her. She had either gotten physically tired, or she reckoned that it was the moment to experience the orgasm; or perhaps it appears to me that the male caught her in a position that she could not escape. The male had his feet on her tail and she fluttered but could not escape. And then she wanted to have it. He made couple of moves and he was done. While the pre coitus took like four minutes, the act itself took just like four seconds.

After the coitus it was totally different. All that hide and go seek was nowhere. The two did not move at all. The female turned 180 degrees, faced the male, sat on the opposite end of the same leaf, and in a position that was more like lying down than standing on the leaf; she laid there completely motionless. He stood more or less where he was during the coitus, except that she was no longer under him; and he too stood there completely motionless. The motionlessness was complete and absolute; nothing of them moved, not the wings, not the feet, not the head – nothing moved at those moments immediately after the coitus. If I could see their eyes, it seemed to me that they did not even wink.

Perhaps they felt they were still in the act of coitus, experiencing the orgasm, over and over in their souls, and perhaps in their minds.

There they were in the state of absolute motionlessness for about six minutes. There was at occasion a gentle breeze, and the leaf would share the ecstasy of the butterflies, perhaps having its own intercourse with the breeze. After about six minutes, I saw the head of the male move ever so gently and minutely, while she just lay there, still

166

motionless. Within few seconds the male flew, about five feet away, and sat down on a tiny twig in the water. She followed him, trying to sit next to him, but there was no space on the tiny twig for her, and she sat down like few inches nearby, facing him. They sat there, and then they did another act of quiet playfulness. The male opened his wings and closed them. He repeated the act couple of times. She caught on with him and did the same. Then one would open the wings and close them, and the other would follow. This continued for couple of minutes.

And then another male butterfly came. I thought that the new comer had come to join them. The female flew and I thought she was flying with him; rather, she was gently trying to persuade him to leave. Then the three of them were flying together, in a rather fast whirlwind sort of pattern. Soon she sat down on the same twig, and the male drove the new comer away – not sure what technique he used but the new comer left. The male returned and sat on the twig. The intruder returned after about thirty seconds, took a round around the two but decided to leave. He returned in another less than a minute, and this time the male flew and drove him away again. The male came and sat back on the twig. The intruder did not return.

They were there for about ten minutes. The female flew and sat on a branch near the leaf on which they had enjoyed their coitus. She stayed there waiting. In about thirty seconds, he two flew and sat on the same branch. There they sat next to each other. They sat there without apparent activity. They were there what seemed like a long time, may be half an hour or even longer. They sat there as if in meditation, as if amusing about what they had just accomplished together.

Finally, the male flew away, I am not sure where he sat. She kept sitting where she was; she sat there, perhaps expecting that he will return – but he did not return. She flew in a soft leisurely orbit and sat down on a branch on the other side of the creek, perhaps in view of him where he was sitting. But he did not return.

I wonder if they would recognize each other when they came across again; after all, they perhaps live in the same neighborhood of the creek. If they meet again, what would they say to each other, what would they do together, if anything?

My coffee was finished, I got up and returned. They were both somewhere there, each sitting on some branch, or taking a flight over the waters, in the breeze.

Appendix A

A Dream and Aftermath

Woke up just before Fajar time at about 5:20 am[52]. It was Friday morning. I had had a dream that left me very sad and perturbed. I dreamed that my mother had died. The place was not in USA but it looked more like our E-56 house at Karachi Air Port. There were miscellaneous things in the foreground, a bed, a bicycle, few obstacles like a box or little things that I did not explicitly recognize. It was night time. Apparently, everyone was asleep. My mother was also presumably asleep. I did not see any faces, only heard the voices.

While asleep, I heard a voice saying something like, wait till she dies and go to sleep for now. I remember hearing it very clearly, in fact this voice is the clearest thing in the dream, and most dominating. But I too did not wake up; and in the morning when I did wake up, that voice was foremost in my consciousness. I asked: is she dead? No one answered. I tended to presume that she was dead; and I started to cry and went into something like convulsions. In this dream, I did not see anyone but I was completely shaken up and deeply lost and aggrieved (I have no words for how it was).

Then I woke up from the dream, and went to the toilet. Went back to bed. But the grief and calamity were with me. In this situation,

---

[52] Bowie, MD: February 26, 2016. 022616.

I lay in bed. As my mother had died on the midnight of May 18, 2001, my first thought, upon waking up, was that it was someone dear to me whose death it was that I experienced in my dream. First, I thought that it was about my elder brother, then it occurred to me that it was about Yasmeen. I stayed there in bed, in a greatly depressed state but tears did not come to me, which is rather unusual for me.

Then I got up and went out to the living room. It was 5:25am. Yasmeen was up on the JaNamaaz for Tahajjud. I stood there gazing, at nothing in particular, under the duress but not thinking much, just experiencing the moment. Then her phone started the Fajar Azaan. I thought of going back, but then the words of the Azaan attracted me, and I stayed on till it was complete. I felt I could not go back to sleep after hearing that Salaat is better than sleep. I stood there contemplating doing the Wudu and doing the Salaat. After sometime she commented: what is it? I told her that in my dream my mother died. She commented it is due to the thoughts; and after a pause she commented that maybe it is her (Yasmeen) who is to die. It was already on my mind, and the thought intensified. I thought of sitting close to her, perhaps on the single sofa; but I sat next to her JaNamaaz on the floor. I sat there thinking nothing, saying nothing, but overcome by feelings. Yasmeen started her Fajar. I touched her foot with affection as she stood in Qiyam. After the Salat she turned to me and at this time I broke into tears, falling my head into her lap as she sat in AttaHyat position. I stayed there what seems like a long time, but may be 5 minutes. It occurred to me that I could not take her passing away, and I asked her not to go. She asked where and I said nowhere, then commenting that I want to pass away before her. She calmly said that it is up to Allah. Then she got up and got me some tissue paper. I went back into her lap and stayed there again, then she suggested that she will bring some water and tea for me. But I stayed there, just stayed, not thinking much, but thoughts came to me. It occurred to me that we become heedless; we do not take note of those we love. Like in the dream, the voice said, let her die and go to sleep till then. I thought we should always remain attentive to those we love, in fact to everyone.

It then occurred to me that my writing the book was something unnecessary for my happiness and wellbeing, partly because it takes my attention away from those I love.

Man is in the best state as he is born; every change in that best state is mostly a change towards degradation. Most human activity is a degradation except the elementary activities of sustenance, and except the few that we do that enhance that pristine state in which we were born. Elementary activities that our inside suggests to us are not degradations. Activities promoted by the society are mostly degradations; even education is degradation, and scientific discoveries are a degradation as they are steered by the society. People who stay at the elementary level are closest to the perfect state they were at birth. Most others have degraded.

Then Yasmeen brought some water and three badaam (almonds) and three kali mirch (black papers) which she gives me these days for few days now. Then she went and made a cup of tea and brought it for me, suggesting I get up and sit on the Sofa. I sat on the Sofa. She made a cup for herself and also brought some walnut and Ritz cookies. After wards we went back to bed.

It was "experiential". Thoughts came to me without thinking, observing, analyzing. All thoughts seemed very clear at that time. If a question arose in my mind, its answer came up spontaneously; again, in an experiential mode.

It is now 10:32 am and I have finished writing this.

My Nani

Couple of days back I had a dream[53]. My Nani (maternal grandmother) came in my dream, like she was in her life. She was dressed in light color dress, talked normally, behaved normally as she used to. She was holding a small bundle wrapped in a white cloth and knotted, like they normally do for a "pand". During the interaction with my Nani, out of curiosity, I unknotted the tiny bundle.

The outer clothe was like a shameez (under shirt for a woman), white in color, very clean except for some brownish water sogging mark at the bottom, and a similar mark, slightly more spread out, at the top. Within the bundle was a white pajama, underneath was an old pantaloon of mine of slightly pale greyish color which I still have and is like a pajama. Then there was a pair of surmai (greyish black) socks which were like my socks; and there was a white small piece, perhaps a handkerchief. May be there was another clothe. Everything was nicely washed, dried, and pressed – very well taken care of.

Her carrying just a few clothes in a nicely done tiny bundle and holding it in her hand suggested to me that the clothes that Yasmeen sends every Ramadan did not reach her. Later, I reminded Yasmeen of

---

[53] Bowie, MD: Wednesday, February 22, 2017.

the situation, and suggested that she confirm from her contact in Pakistan that the clothes were actually given in khairat (charity).

Lost in a village

Before waking up at around 8:30 am, I had this dream for what seems like over an hour[54]. I am in a small room, presumably in a one-room-hostel like thing in the middle of strange farm fields, and about quarter mile from a village. The field does not have plants but a lineout of what looked like pieces of earthen ware, laid out in the whole field like as if they were plants. It is a tiny room with a bed and perhaps nothing else. The bed blocks the door, which has no lock; the bed itself stops it from opening.

The room is on a one lane paved road. There is no one in the vicinity. It is as if the room stands there by itself, with may be a small adjoining structure which I did not see, and there was no one else.

I went out on the road and I could see the village at few hundred yards to the left of the room. In front was the road; in the back was the field of broken earthen pots as I described above, with pieces of earthenware instead of plants. I am thinking I will go to the village and get some help, may be a taxi that will take me home, or someplace where I can get transport for home.

Then I find myself near the fields; and I am on the phone with home; there is only Adnan on the phone, and Yasmeen; there is no one

---

[54] Bowie, MD: February 20, 2022.

else at home. Adnan points out that there are lot of voices he hears on the phone. And there is of course no one, but the "plants" of earthenware are somehow making sounds as if singing. I thought I recognized an English word from the song.

I am talking to Adnan, perhaps to come and get me; but also saying that I will go to the village and try to get some help. I am not without money, and I am not in panic, but there is some distress. Yasmeen tries to tell me not to talk of the distress to Adnan so as not to distress him.

Then I find myself in a place where there is a meeting of villagers discussing BJP misbehavior and also having a meeting with some local Hindu leader. After that there are people praying. Some remarking against meeting with Hindu leader at the occasion of prayer. Then they are praying and I am trying to get out of the room, and not being able to reach the door, or something; the path beyond from the door is also muddied up or something; apparently there are more than one door out of what seemed like a circular mud place; but all doors seemed muddied up.

Reality and Dreams

I often have dreams; they are not pleasant[55]. Often, they are like real life situations, the situations are often of a type of difficulty. For example, I had a dream last night. I was at an airport, perhaps somewhere in Germany. I was perhaps resuming a flight after a layover. At the counter, which is a girl standing at an arbitrary place, like someone giving guidance, I could not find my passport, nor my boarding pass. After a little while someone wrote for me a hand written boarding pass. I took a train to reach the boarding gate; it seems the boarding gates were spread out like cities in a province. There were trains constantly running from gate 1 to gate 217, for example. I got down at a stop. The bottom ladder, while getting down, caught my foot, as if by a magnetic type force, and I fell down. Some passenger asked if I had purchased the ticket, and I replied no, implying that I was not aware I needed a ticket. An official appeared and said he will take care of it. And he used some sort of key to release my foot.

The train left and I found myself stranded. Soon I lost sense of the direction as to which trains were going towards gate 1 and which direction was going towards gate 217. I asked around but I did not find the answer. Then I asked someone again and he did not know and was

---

[55] Bowie, MD: Tuesday, April 2nd, 2019.

trying to guess, and there was a taxi standing there, as if at a crossing over the train tracks. I asked the guy to ask the taxi driver if he knew, but, instead, they negotiated a rate to go to gate 217 by taxi. It was 20 pesos. I gathered traffic would be slow on the roads and I might miss my flight. So, I said no to the taxi, and he reduced the price to 10.5.

Then I started walking into the train tunnel. After few yards, I saw a train coming. I decided to get out of the way of the train. The clearance from the tunnel wall was just enough for the train to pass, so I gathered I could not stand on that side. I decided to go to the area between the train tracks, that was twice as wide. But then I saw another train coming in the opposite direction on the second tracks. Now there was no place for me to stand. So, I panicked and started running back towards the crossing point where I was earlier. As I was running, I could not lift my legs; this happens sometimes in my dreams that my legs do not move and I have to lift them with my hands to take the next step.

Dreams are realistic, containing familiar things and situations and occurrences. It is as if it is really happening. It exerts the biological and psychological impacts on the dreamer, same impact as would be experienced in a real-life situation. The only difference is that one quickly realizes upon waking up that it was only a dream. Until one wakes up the situation in the dream is real. Like my Nani used to say: Sufne da Baghyard na Sadde jad tak jagein nahin (until you wake up, the wolf chasing you would not stop).

So, what is the difference between the dream and a reality?

The difference is made manifest by the act of waking up; it is not clarified by some logic or reasoning. If one does not wake up, the dream is the reality; and the reality does not exist. The difference made by the waking up is the experience of the real world that invalidates the experience in the dream because it does not continue to be persistent. For a person who does not wake up, the dream is persistent, and the experience of reality is absent. For such a person the dream and reality interchange their significance.

This situation also happens in the real world itself. The non-persistence of an experience can manifest during travels. Experience of one country and one culture ceases and the experience of another country and culture begins. If one does it a lot, the mind treats these non-persistent experiences like it treats the dreams. For example, during three months of travels I experienced USA-Mexico-Guatemala-Honduras-USA. When I returned, I did not know where I was and the significance of events, even the very grave ones, did not impact me in the usual way.

So, dreams make us aware of situations and happenings that are possible though we may never experience them because we do not cross certain boundaries that may cause those situations to arise. In this sense dreams are like traveling and experiencing situations that we may never experience otherwise. In some sense, dreams are the realities of another set of boundary conditions and another configuration of the phase space within which we live.

It would appear that there is no concrete difference between reality and dreams – dreams are reality and reality are dreams of a different set of boundary conditions and phase space configurations.

Made in the USA
Middletown, DE
09 August 2023

36301656R00116